EVERYMAN,
I WILL GO WITH THEE
AND BE THY GUIDE,
IN THY MOST NEED
TO GO BY THY SIDE

EVERYMAN'S LIBRARY
POCKET POETS

# *FAIRY POEMS*

EDITED BY
LYNNE GREENBERG

EVERYMAN'S LIBRARY
POCKET POETS

Alfred A. Knopf  New York  London  Toronto

THIS IS A BORZOI BOOK
PUBLISHED BY ALFRED A. KNOPF

This selection by Lynne Greenberg
first published in Everyman's Library, 2023
Copyright © 2023 by Everyman's Library

Second printing (US)

All rights reserved. Published in the United States by Alfred A.
Knopf, a division of Penguin Random House LLC, New York, and
in Canada by Penguin Random House Canada Limited, Toronto.
Distributed by Penguin Random House LLC, New York. Published
in the United Kingdom by Everyman's Library, 50 Albemarle
Street, London W1S 4BD and distributed by Penguin Random
House UK, 20 Vauxhall Bridge Road, London SW1V 2SA.

everymanslibrary.com
www.everymanslibrary.co.uk

ISBN 978-0-593-53629-2 (US)
978-1-84159-829-1 (UK)

A CIP catalogue record for this book is available
from the British Library

Typography by Peter B. Willberg

Typeset in the UK by Input Data Services Ltd,
Isle Abbotts, Somerset

Printed and bound in Germany
by GGP Media GmbH, Pössneck

# CONTENTS

## FAIRY FOLK

## MERMAIDS AND WATER-FOLK

10

## SYMBOLIC FAIRIES

11

# FOREWORD

With deep roots in pagan traditions and religions, fairies are ubiquitous in mythology and folklore in all periods of recorded history. Their wings' breadth spans continents, and anthropologists, ethnographers, and folklorists have traced belief in fairies worldwide.

The origin stories of fairies are diverse. In Irish tradition, fairies were said to have descended from the Tuatha Dé Danann, a superior race of beings and rulers. Others believed that fairies were fallen angels, of neither heaven nor hell. In the seventeenth century, Robert Kirk, one of the first Gaelic folklorists, wrote: "Siths, or Fairies, they call Sluagh Maith, or the Good-people ... are said to be of a middle nature betwixt man and angel, as were demons thought to be of old." To still others, fairies were the descendants of monstrous pre-Christian beings or of Cain. They have alternatively been characterized as restless spirits of the dead. While their origin stories differ, certain attributes of fairies appear in a number of cultures, including superior strength, uncanny intelligence, invisibility, supernatural gifts, and otherworldly physicalities.

Fairies, indeed, are endowed with powerful abilities, one of which is their capacity to soar into every literary genre. Transmitted originally through oral cultures, fairy stories are extant in ballads, songs, myths, and legends. Later, fairies become principal characters in epics, romances, dramas, and lyric poetry. Poets, inspired and haunted by fairies, both benevolent and wicked, have created a lasting canon of fairy poetry. This volume offers a sampling of classic works as well as lesser-known works, including traditional ballads, from a range of genres and places, focusing on the English and Irish traditions. Modern and contemporary poems about fairies attest to their enduring influence at the level of myth.

The poems sing of "Faerie," the enchanted places in which fairies were thought to dwell: Tir Na N'og, the land of youth; Hy-Brasil, the fabled isle of the blessed; Avalon; forest; flower; cairn; body of water; the air itself. "Fairy" as a generic term encompasses a world of creatures, regionally and even locally named. Encyclopedias are devoted to classifying the different fairies, their appearance, behavior, and dwellings. A number of these creatures — elves, pixies, mermaids, and goblins, to name but a few — populate the poems. The characters, from Queen Mab to Robin Goodfellow, are as diverse as the types of fairies. They are kings and queens, helpful domestics, pranksters, muses, lovers, and murderers.

Fairies are liminal creatures. Morally ambivalent and having their own codes of behavior, the "good people" or "gentle folk," as they were euphemistically called in Ireland, have been greeted alternatively with terror, skepticism, and delight. In the Renaissance, Protestant writers decried fairies as satanic beings or illusory manifestations of Satan. In Scotland, an admission of having seen fairies could lead to an accusation of witchcraft. In the seventeenth century, Puritan writers railed against fairy belief as mere superstition. In our time, fairies have been relegated to storybooks and cartoons for children.

The poems in this volume reflect the range of human reactions to fairies. Some revel in fairies' festive activities, their love of dance and song and their guardianship of the natural world. Other poems smile at their mischievous antics. Many of the poems bewail fairies' malevolence. Preternaturally desirable, both male and female fairies were said to beguile, entice, and seduce the unwary. Fairies were also believed to abduct human children, replacing them with changelings, or fairy children, who would not thrive. These leitmotifs appear often in the poetry and suggest our all-too-human efforts to account for tragedy and disaster. In ages when fairies were feared as a mortal threat, humans sought both to channel and to ward off their magic through medicinal recipes, rituals, prayers, and charms. This volume includes a sampling of such poetic spells.

The poems are rich in fae "glamour," that is, the

ability to shape-shift. The poems themselves shift between a range of moods and registers, at times lyrical and whimsical, at other times hypnotic and disturbing. Poets have invoked fairies' transformative ability to explore the endlessly shifting resonances and meanings of the word fairy itself. As early as the nineteenth century, the term was used derogatorily to refer to homosexuals. It since has been reclaimed, in part due to Harry Hay, the founder of the Radical Faeries movement in the 1970s. Poets gesture alternatively, and sometimes in closeted ways, to the sexual valences of the term. A separate section of the volume is devoted to poets who wrote of their experiences with absinthe, popularly referred to as *la feé verte* (the green fairy). Particularly in the late-1900s, absinthe served as a source of inspiration for poets. A number of these poems absorb and are absorbed in the hallucinogenic properties of wormwood. Several of the poems in this volume allude to fairies in symbolic ways: to offer critiques of war, to mourn the passing of youth, and to celebrate the beloved, nature, even the creative imagination itself. The range of poetic uses of fairies suggests the power of their glamour.

In choosing poems for this volume, the only difficulty was in deciding which works to include from amongst the rich traditions. Regardless of author, genre, or place of creation, each poem has been chosen for its timelessness. Together, they speak to our love of story, collective wonderment at the invisible and unknown, and desire to understand the ineffable mysteries of grief, longing, love, and joy. May these fairy poems offer flight. May they lure and allure you.

Lynne Greenberg

# ENCHANTED PLACES

*Faerie is a perilous land, and in it are pitfalls for the unwary and dungeons for the overbold . . . I will not attempt to define that, nor to describe it directly. It cannot be done. Faerie cannot be caught in a net of words; for it is one of its qualities to be indescribable, though not imperceptible.*

J. R. R. TOLKIEN, "On Fairy-Stories" (1947)

## From BALLAD OF THOMAS THE RHYMER

*"O see you not yon narrow road,*
  *So thick beset with thorns and briers? –*
*That is the path of righteousness,*
  *Though after it there's few enquires.*

*"And see ye not yon braid, braid road,*
  *That lies across yon lily leven?*
*That is the path of wickedness,*
  *Though some call it the road to heaven.*

*"And see ye not that bonny road,*
  *That winds about the fernie brae?*
*That is the road to fair Elfland,*
  *Where thou and I this night maun gae.*

SIR THOMAS DE ERCIDOUN (*c.* 1220–88)
TRANSLATED BY FRANCIS JAMES CHILD

## From A MIDSUMMER NIGHT'S DREAM

I know a bank where the wild thyme blows,
Where oxlips and the nodding violet grows,
Quite over-canopied with luscious woodbine,
With sweet musk-roses and with eglantine:
There sleeps Titania sometime of the night,
Lull'd in these flowers with dances and delight;
And there the snake throws her enamell'd skin,
Weed wide enough to wrap a fairy in . . .

WILLIAM SHAKESPEARE (1564– 1616)

# HY-BRASAIL – THE ISLE OF THE BLEST

On the ocean that hollows the rocks where ye dwell,
A shadowy land has appeared, as they tell;
Men thought it a region of sunshine and rest,
And they called it *Hy-Brasail*, the isle of the blest.
From year unto year on the ocean's blue rim,
The beautiful spectre showed lovely and dim;
The golden clouds curtained the deep where it lay,
And it looked like an Eden, away, far away!

A peasant who heard of the wonderful tale,
In the breeze of the Orient loosened his sail;
From Ara, the holy, he turned to the west,
For though Ara was holy, *Hy-Brasail* was blest.
He heard not the voices that called from the shore –
He heard not the rising wind's menacing roar;
Home, kindred, and safety, he left on that day,
And he sped to *Hy-Brasail*, away, far away!

Morn rose on the deep, and that shadowy isle,
O'er the faint rim of distance, reflected its smile;
Noon burned on the wave, and that shadowy shore
Seemed lovelily distant, and faint as before;
Lone evening came down on the wanderer's track,
And to Ara again he looked timidly back;

Oh! far on the verge of the ocean it lay,
Yet the isle of the blest was away, far away!

Rash dreamer, return! O, ye winds of the main,
Bear him back to his own peaceful Ara again.
Rash fool! for a vision of fanciful bliss,
To barter thy calm life of labour and peace.
The warning of reason was spoken in vain;
He never revisited Ara again!
Night fell on the deep, amidst tempest and spray,
And he died on the waters, away, far away!

GERALD GRIFFIN (1803−40)

## From THE LAY OF OISIN IN THE LAND OF YOUTH

"Delightful land beyond all dreams!
  Beyond what seems to thee most fair –
  Rich fruits abound the bright year round
  And flowers are found of hues most rare.

"Unfailing there the honey and wine
  And draughts divine of mead there be,
  No ache nor ailing night or day –
  Death or decay thou ne'er shalt see!

"The mirthful feast and joyous play
  And music's sway all blest, benign –
  Silver untold and store of gold
  Undreamt by the old shall all be thine!

"A hundred swords of steel refined
  A hundred cloaks of kind full rare,
  A hundred steeds of proudest breed
  A hundred hounds – thy meed when there!

"A hundred coats of mail shall be thine
  A hundred kine of sleekest skin,
  A hundred sheep with fleece of gold
  And gems none hold these shores within.

"A hundred maidens young and fair
    Of blithesome air shall tend on thee,
    Of form most meet, as fairies fleet
    And of song more sweet than the wild thrush free!

"A hundred knights in fights most bold
    Of skill untold in all chivalrie,
    Full-armed, bedight in mail of gold
    Shall in *Tír na n-Óg* thy comrades be.

"A corslet charmed for thee shall be made
    And a matchless blade of magic power,
    Worth a hundred blades in a hero's hands,
    Most blest of brands in battle's hour!

"The royal crown of the King of Youth
    Shall shine in sooth on thy brow most fair,
    All brilliant with gems of lustre bright
    Whose worth aright none might declare."

MICHAEL COIMÍN (1688–1760)                    25

# THE FAËRY FOREST

The faëry forest glimmered
  Beneath an ivory moon,
The silver grasses shimmered
  Against a faëry tune.

Beneath the silken silence
  The crystal branches slept,
And dreaming through the dew-fall
  The cold, white blossoms wept.

# IN THE WOOD OF FINVARA

I have grown tired of sorrow and human tears;
Life is a dream in the night, a fear among fears,
A naked runner lost in a storm of spears.

I have grown tired of rapture and love's desire;
Love is a flaming heart, and its flames aspire
Till they cloud the soul in the smoke of a windy fire.

I would wash the dust of the world in a soft green
    flood;
Here between sea and sea, in the fairy wood,
I have found a delicate, wave-green solitude.

Here, in the fairy wood, between sea and sea,
I have heard the song of a fairy bird in a tree,
And the peace that is not in the world has flown
    to me.

ARTHUR SYMONS (1865–1945)                                    27

## From SIR ORFEO

In at a rock the ladies rode,
   And fearlessly he followed fast.
When far into the rock he strode,
   It grew more bright, and so at last
   Into a far countree he passed,
Bright as the fairest summer sun:
   All smooth and plain and green and vast,
For hills and valleys were there none.

Amid the land a castle tall
   And rich and proud and wondrous high
Uprose, and all the outmost wall
   Shone as a crystal to the eye.
   A hundred towers lit up the sky,
Of diamond all battled stout;
   And buttresses rose up near by
Arched with red gold and broad about.

All the bonsour was carved in stone
   With every beast and every wight,
And all within the castle shone
   And sparkled with unearthly light.
   The meanest pillars to the sight
Seemed every whit of burnished gold.

And all that land was warm and bright,
For when our earth is dark and cold,

The jewelled stones shed forth a light
  Like sunbeams on a summer's day.
None may describe that wondrous sight
  Or sculptured work so proud and gay;
  But one would think that rich array
Were of the courts of Paradise.
  Therein the ladies led the way;
He followed fast in sweet surprise.

ANONYMOUS (*c.* 13TH–14TH CENTURY)          29
TRANSLATED BY EDWARD EYRE HUNT

# From NYMPHIDIA: THE FAIRY COURT

This palace standeth in the air,
By necromancy placed there,
That it no tempests needs to fear,
    Which way soe'er it blow it;
And somewhat southward toward the noon,
Whence lies a way up to the moon,
And thence the Fairy can as soon
    Pass to the earth below it.
The walls of spiders' legs are made
Well mortised and finely laid;
He was the master of his trade
    It curiously that builded;
The windows of the eyes of cats,
And for the roof, instead of slats,
Is covered with the skins of bats,
    With moonshine that are gilded.

# THE WELL OF ALL HEALING

There's a cure for all things in the well at Ballylee
    Where the scarlet cressets hang over the
        trembling pool:
And joyful winds are blowing from the Land of Youth
        to me,
    And the heart of the earth is full.

Many and many a sunbright maiden saw the
        enchanted land
    With star faces glimmer up from the druid wave:
Many and many a pain of love was soothed by a
        faery hand
    Or lost in the love it gave.

When the quiet with a ring of pearl shall wed the
        earth,
    And the scarlet berries burn dark by the stars in
        the pool;
Oh, it's lost and deep I'll be amid the windy mirth,
    While the heart of the earth is full.

A. E. (GEORGE WILLIAM RUSSELL) (1867–1935)     31

# THE FOUNTAIN OF THE FAIRIES

There is a fountain in the forest call'd
The Fountain of the Fairies: when a child
With a delightful wonder I have heard
Tales of the elfin tribe who on its banks
Hold midnight revelry. An ancient oak,
The goodliest of the forest, grows beside;
Alone it stands, upon a green grass plat,
By the woods bounded like some little isle.
It ever hath been deem'd their favourite tree.
They love to lie and rock upon its leaves,
And bask in moonshine. Here the woodman leads
His boy, and showing him the green-sward mark'd
With darker circlets, says the midnight dance
Hath traced the rings, and bids him spare the tree.
Fancy had cast a spell upon the place
Which made it holy; and the villagers
Would say that never evil thing approach'd
Unpunish'd there. The strange and fearful pleasure
Which fill'd me by that solitary spring,
Ceased not in riper years; and now it wakes
Deeper delight, and more mysterious awe.

## LOVELY LADY
(*Mir's Wooing of Éadaoin*)

Lovely lady will you go
To that kingdom where stars glow?
   Primrose there the colour of hair
   Snow white each body fair.

"Yours" and "mine" are words not known yet,
Ivory teeth and brows of pure jet:
   Foxglove the colour of every cheek,
   The whole company radiant and sleek.

Every plain of purple hue,
The blackbird's eggs flecked with blue,
   The plains of Ireland will seem bare
   After you have lingered there.

For Ireland's beer you will not long,
The Great Land's beer is twice as strong!
   It is a land of purest gold,
   The young don't die before the old.

All round gentle stream entwine,
Mead is drunk, the best of wine;
   The people have not learned to hate,
   It's not a sin to copulate!

We see all on every side
Though none sees us – we do not hide
　　But Adam's sin has caused a cloak
　　Between us and ordinary folk.

Woman, if you come with me,
On your head a crown will be,
　　Fresh pork, milk, the finest ale
　　Await us now beyond the pale.

TRANSLATED BY GABRIEL ROSENSTOCK

## From KILMENY

Bonnie Kilmeny gaed up the glen;
But it wasna to meet Duneira's men,
Nor the rosy monk of the isle to see,
For Kilmeny was pure as pure could be.
It was only to hear the yorling sing,
And pu' the cress-flower round the spring;
The scarlet hypp and the hind-berrye,
And the nest that hung frae the hazel-tree;
For Kilmeny was pure as pure could be.
But lang may her minny look o'er the wa';
And lang may she seek i' the greenwood shaw;
Lang the Laird o' Duneira blame,
And lang, lang greet or Kilmeny come hame!

When many lang day had come and fled,
When grief grew calm and hope was dead,
When mass for Kilmeny's soul had been sung,
When the bedesman had prayed and the dead-bell
    rung,
Late, late in a gloaming, when all was still,
When the fringe was red on the westlin hill,
The wood was sere, the moon i' the wane,
The reek o' the cot hung o'er the plain,
Like a little wee cloud in the world its lane;

When the ingle lowed wi' an eiry leme –
Late, late in the gloaming, Kilmeny came hame!

"Kilmeny, Kilmeny, where have you been?
Lang hae we sought baith holt and dean;
By burn, by ford, by greenwood tree,
Yet you are halesome and fair to see.
Where gat ye that joup o' the lily sheen?
That bonnie snood o' the birk sae green?
And those roses, the fairest that ever were seen?
Kilmeny, Kilmeny, where have you been?"

Kilmeny look'd up wi' a lovely grace,
But nae smile was seen on Kilmeny's face;
As still was her look, and as still was her e'e,
As the stillness that lay on the emerant lea,
Or the mist that sleeps on a waveless sea.
For Kilmeny had been, she kenned not where,
And Kilmeny had seen what she could not declare;
Killmeny had been where the cock never crew,
Where the rain never fell, and the wind never blew.

But it seemed as the harp of the sky had rung,
And the airs of heaven played round her tongue,
When she spoke of the lovely forms she had seen,
And a land where sin had never been;

A land of love and a land of light,
Withouten sun, or moon, or night,
Where the river swa'd a living stream,
And the light a pure and cloudless beam;
The land of vision it would seem,
A still, an everlasting dream.

JAMES HOGG (1770—1835)

# THE VOYAGERS

We shall launch our shallop on waters blue from some
    dim primrose shore,
We shall sail with the magic of dusk behind and
    enchanted coasts before,
Over oceans that stretch to the sunset land where lost
    Atlantis lies,
And our pilot shall be the vesper star that shines in
    the amber skies.

The sirens will call to us again, all sweet and demon-fair,
And a pale mermaiden will beckon us, with mist on
    her night-black hair;
We shall see the flash of her ivory arms, her mocking
    and luring face,
And her guiling laughter will echo through the great,
    wind-winnowed space.

But we shall not linger for woven spell, or sea-
    nymph's sorceries,
It is ours to seek for the fount of youth, and the gold
    of Hesperides,
Till the harp of the waves in its rhythmic beat keeps
    time to our pulses' swing,
And the orient welkin is smit to flame with auroral
    crimsoning.

And at last, on some white and wondrous dawn, we
    shall reach the fairy isle
Where our hope and our dream are waiting us, and
    the to-morrows smile;
With song on our lips and faith in our hearts we sail
    on our ancient quest,
And each man shall find, at the end of the voyage, the
    thing he loves the best.

## ST. ANDREW'S

While the sun was going down,
There arose a fairy town.

Not the town I saw by day,
Cheerless, joyless, dull, and gray;

But a far, fantastic place,
Builded with ethereal grace,

Shimmering in a tender mist
That the slanting rays had kissed,

Ere they let their latest fire
Touch with gold each slender spire.

There no men and women be:
Mermen, maidens of the sea,

Combing out their tangled locks,
Sit and sing among the rocks.

As their ruddy harps they sound,
With the seaweed twisted round,

In the shining sand below
See the city downward go!

# THE BERRY HOLLOW OF LAG NA SMÉAR

Here are blackberries
in seductive clusters
in heavy tresses

Numberless berries
soaked in the earth's blood
and fired by the sun

Neat produce of tangled briars;
soft juice of autumnal days
wayside banquet

There they hang,
full of lure blushing purple –
a generous spread

My passions are aroused
and prick me as they like
I must have them!

Wild and bloodthirsty
a matter of life and death
each juicy mouthful

I cannot overcome their charms!
every year I plunge my fangs
into their pulsing veins

Their sweet soft bloodiness.
To pass them by
without tasting them

Would send me into paroxysms
of starvation.
Delicious, swollen, lascivious

I fondle them
in the palm of my hand.
Demon of Gluttony am I

The vampire
that licks their pulchritude
with blood-smeared tongue

And how miserable I am
when their sheen is gone
when old age disfigures them

As November drags on
the fairy people do their business
and the bushes stink to the high heavens

42   CATHAL Ó SEARCAIGH (1956–)
TRANSLATED BY GABRIEL ROSENSTOCK

# FAIRY FOLK

*But supposing they actually do exist, what are these creatures?*

SIR ARTHUR CONAN DOYLE, upon seeing the Cottingley fairy photographs (1922)

*Fairies here your steps advance;*
*To the harp's soft dulcet sound,*
*Let your footsteps lightly bound.*
*Unveil your forms to mortal eye.*

FELICIA DOROTHEA HEMANS,
"Invocation to the Fairies" (1812)

## From *THE FAERIE QUEENE*

*. . . Prometheus did create*
*A man, of many parts from beasts deryv'd,*
*And then stole fire from heven to animate*
*His worke, for which he was by Iove depryv'd*
*Of life himselfe, and hart-strings of an aegle ryv'd.*

*That man so made he called Elfe, to weet*
*Quick, the first author of all Elfin kynd;*
*Who, wandring through the world with wearie feet,*
*Did in the gardins of Adonis fynd*
*A goodly creature, whom he deemd in mynd*
*To be no earthly wight, but either spright,*
*Or angell, th' authour of all woman kynd;*
*Therefore a Fay he her according hight,*
*Of whom all Faryes spring, and fetch their lignage right.*

EDMUND SPENSER (1552−99)

## From TAM LIN

But we that live in Fairyland
No sickness know, nor pain;
I quit my body when I will,
And take to it again.
Our shapes and size we can convert
To either large or small,
An old nut-shell's the same to us
As is the lofty hall.
We sleep in rose-buds soft and sweet,
We revel in the stream,
We wanton lightly on the wind,
Or glide on a sunbeam.

SIR WALTER SCOTT (1771 – 1832)

## THE DISCOVERY

These are the days of elfs and fays:
Who says that with the dreams of myth,
These imps and elves disport themselves?
Ah no, along the paths of song
Do all the tiny folk belong.

Round all our homes,
Kobolds and gnomes do daily cling,
Then nightly fling their lanterns out.
And shout on shout, they join the rout,
And sing, and sing, within the sweet enchanted ring.

Where gleamed the guile of moonlight's smile,
Once paused I, listening for a while,
And heard the lay, unknown by day, –
The fairies' dancing roundelay.

Queen Mab was there, her shimmering hair
Each fairy prince's heart's despair.
She smiled to see their sparkling glee,
And once I ween, she smiled at me.

Since when, you may by night or day,
Dispute the sway of elf-folk gay;
But, hear me, stay!
I've learned the way to find Queen Mab and elf
    and fay.

Where e'er by streams, the moonlight gleams,
Or on a meadow softly beams,
There, footing round on dew-lit ground,
The fairy folk may all be found.

# THE FAIRY HOST

Pure white the shields their arms upbear,
With silver emblems rare o'ercast;
Amid blue glittering blades they go,
The horns they blow are loud of blast.

In well-instructed ranks of war
Before their Chief they proudly pace;
Coerulean spears o'er every crest –
A curly-tressed, pale-visaged race.

Beneath the flame of their attack,
Bare and black turns every coast;
With such a terror to the fight
Flashes that mighty vengeful host.

Small wonder that their strength is great,
Since royal in estate are all,
Each hero's head a lion's fell –
A golden yellow mane lets fall.

Comely and smooth their bodies are,
Their eyes the starry blue eclipse,
The pure white crystal of their teeth
Laughs out beneath their thin red lips.

Good are they at man-slaying feats,
Melodious over meats and ale;
Of woven verse they wield the spell,
At chess-craft they excel the Gael.

ANONYMOUS (*c.* 8TH CENTURY)

TRANSLATED BY ALFRED PERCIVAL GRAVES

# TO THE LEANÁN SIDHE

Where is thy lovely perilous abode?
   In what strange phantom-land
Glimmer the fairy turrets whereto rode
   The ill-starred poet band?

Say, in the Isle of Youth hast thou thy home,
   The sweetest singer there,
Stealing on wingéd steed across the foam
   Through the moonlit air?

Or, where the mists of bluebell float beneath
   The red stems of the pine,
And sunbeams strike thro' shadow, dost thou breathe
   The word that makes him thine?

Or by the gloomy peaks of Erigal,
   Haunted by storm and cloud,
Wing past, and to thy lover there let fall
   His singing-robe and shroud?

Or, is thy palace entered thro' some cliff
   When radiant tides are full,
And round thy lover's wandering, starlit skiff,
   Coil in luxurious lull?

And would he entering on the brimming flood,
    See caverns vast in height,
And diamond columns, crowned with leaf and bud,
    Glow in long lanes of light,

And there, the pearl of that great glittering shell
    Trembling, behold thee lone,
Now weaving in slow dance an awful spell,
    Now still upon thy throne?

Thy beauty! ah, the eyes that pierce him thro'
    Then melt as in a dream;
The voice that sings the mysteries of the blue
    And all that Be and Seem!

Thy lovely motions answering to the rhyme
    That ancient Nature sings,
That keeps the stars in cadence for all time,
    And echoes thro' all things!

Whether he sees thee thus, or in his dreams,
    Thy light makes all lights dim;
An aching solitude from henceforth seems
    The world of men to him.

Thy luring song, above the sensuous roar,
   He follows with delight,
Shutting behind him Life's last gloomy door,
   And fares into the Night.

# THE ELVES

Elves are no smaller
than men, and walk
as men do, in this world,
but with more grace than most,
and are not immortal.

Their beauty sets them aside
from other men and from women
unless a woman has that cold fire in her
called poet: with that

she may see them and by its light
they know her and are not afraid
and silver tongues of love
flicker between them.

DENISE LEVERTOV (1923–97)

## From ROMEO AND JULIET

O, then, I see Queen Mab hath been with you.
She is the fairies' midwife, and she comes
In shape no bigger than an agate-stone
On the fore-finger of an alderman,
Drawn with a team of little atomies
Athwart men's noses as they lie asleep;
Her waggon-spokes made of long spinners' legs,
The cover of the wings of grasshoppers,
The traces of the smallest spider's web,
The collars of the moonshine's watery beams,
Her whip of cricket's bone, the lash of film,
Her waggoner a small grey-coated gnat,
Not half so big as a round little worm
Prick'd from the lazy finger of a maid;
Her chariot is an empty hazel-nut
Made by the joiner squirrel or old grub,
Time out o' mind the fairies' coachmakers.
And in this state she gallops night by night
Through lovers' brains, and then they dream of love;
O'er courtiers' knees, that dream on court'sies
        straight,
O'er lawyers' fingers, who straight dream on fees,
O'er ladies' lips, who straight on kisses dream,
Which oft the angry Mab with blisters plagues,
Because their breaths with sweetmeats tainted are:

Sometime she gallops o'er a courtier's nose,
And then dreams he of smelling out a suit;
And sometime comes she with a tithe-pig's tail
Tickling a parson's nose as a' lies asleep,
Then dreams he of another benefice:
Sometime she driveth o'er a soldier's neck,
And then dreams he of cutting foreign throats,
Of breaches, ambuscadoes, Spanish blades,
Of healths five-fathom deep; and then anon
Drums in his ear, at which he starts and wakes,
And being thus frighted swears a prayer or two
And sleeps again. This is that very Mab
That plats the manes of horses in the night,
And bakes the elf-locks in foul sluttish hairs,
Which once untangled much misfortune bodes:
This is she —

## From QUEEN MAB; A PHILOSOPHICAL POEM

I am the Fairy Mab: to me 'tis given
The wonders of the human world to keep:
The secrets of the immeasurable past,
In the unfailing consciences of men,
Those stern, unflattering chroniclers, I find:
The future, from the causes which arise
In each event, I gather: not the sting
Which retributive memory implants
In the hard bosom of the selfish man;
Nor that extatic and exulting throb
Which virtue's votary feels when he sums up
The thoughts and actions of a well-spent day,
Are unforeseen, unregistered by me:
And it is yet permitted me, to rend
The veil of mortal frailty, that the spirit
Clothed in its changeless purity, may know
How soonest to accomplish the great end
For which it hath its being, and may taste
That peace, which in the end all life will share.
This is the meed of virtue; happy Soul,
    Ascend the car with me!

## A FAIRY

Call my fairy what you will,
Urgèle, or Morgana, still
I would have her in a dream,
All transparent though she seem,
Come to me with drooping head,
Like a flower that's well-nigh dead.

Musically, from the strings
Of her ivory lute she brings,
Back to me, the wondrous store
Which the paladins of yore
From their history could unfold –
Wilder than the tales they told.

She it is who brings me near
To the things I should revere;
At her bidding I am bound
On the well-tuned harp to sound
All a minstrel's love-songs bright,
With the gauntlet of a knight.

In the desert when I stray,
From my loved home far away,
Hiding there herself I find,
Making ever in my mind,

From each sunbeam, love's bright flame,
From each echo, some dear name.

Hark! she murmurs in the shock
Of the wild wave on the rock;
She to please me with a gift
Doth the silvered stork uplift,
Shining with its plumage white,
From the belfry's topmost height.

When my winter log is lit,
By the chimney-side she'll sit,
And will show my wondering gaze
In the sky a meteor's blaze,
Which will shine out and then die,
Like a slumberer's drowsy eye.

When the cradle of my race,
In our ancient haunts I trace,
With a thousand forms of fear
She enshrouds me far and near,
Like a cataract of sound
In the caverns underground.

If at night I sleepless lie,
She will soothing thoughts supply,
Thoughts of chase and baying hound,
Mellowed by the distant sound,
Echoes of the bugle played
In the depths of forest glade.

# THE BANSHEE

Now God between us and all harm,
    For I to-night have seen
A banshee in the shadow pass
    Along the dark boreen.

And as she went she keened and cried
    And combed her long white hair,
She stopped at Molly Reilly's door,
    And sobbed till midnight there.

And is it for himself she moans,
    Who is so far away?
Or is it Molly Reilly's death
    She cries until the day?

Now Molly thinks her man is gone
    A sailor lad to be;
She puts a candle at her door
    Each night for him to see.

But he is off to Galway town,
    (And who dare tell her this?)
Enchanted by a woman's eyes,
    Half-maddened by her kiss.

So as we go by Molly's door
   We look towards the sea,
And say, "May God bring home your lad,
   Wherever he may be."

I pray it may be Molly's self
   The banshee keens and cries,
For who dare breathe the tale to her,
   Be it her man who dies?

But there is sorrow on the way,
   For I to-night have seen
A banshee in the shadow pass
   Along the dark boreen.

## VILAS

Vishnia! lovely vishnia!
Lift thy branches higher;
For beneath thy branches,
Vilas dance delighted:
While Radisha dashes
From the flow'rs the dewdrops.
Vilas two conveying.
To the third he whispers:
"O be mine, sweet Vila!
Thou, with mine own mother,
In the shade shalt seat thee;
Silken vestments spinning,
Weaving golden garments."

ANONYMOUS, SERBIAN TRADITIONAL POEM
(c. 7TH CENTURY)
TRANSLATED BY JOHN BOWRING

# THE PÚCA

The Púca's come again,
Who long was hid away
In cave or twilight glen:
Too shy, too proud to play
Under the eye of day.

I saw him dance and skip
But now in the beech wood,
Wild rhymes upon his lip
And laughter in his blood.
I envied him his grip
Upon the sunny mood.

Then altered he his note
To one of weariness:
He shook his hairy coat,
The double of distress,
And cried deep in his throat
For gall and bitterness.

The Púca's gone again
To sleep his wits away
In cave or twilight glen:
Too shy, too proud to stay
Under the eye of day.

JOSEPH CAMPBELL (1879–1944)                    63

## From IDYLLS OF THE KING

"And there I saw mage Merlin, whose vast wit
And hundred winters are but as the hands
Of loyal vassals toiling for their liege.

"And near him stood the Lady of the Lake,
Who knows a subtler magic than his own –
Clothed in white samite, mystic, wonderful.
She gave the King his huge cross-hilted sword,
Whereby to drive the heathen out: a mist
Of incense curl'd about her, and her face
Wellnigh was hidden in the minster gloom;
But there was heard among the holy hymns
A voice as of the waters, for she dwells
Down in a deep – calm, whatsoever storms
May shake the world – and when the surface rolls,
Hath power to walk the waters like our Lord.

"There likewise I beheld Excalibur
Before him at his crowning borne, the sword
That rose from out the bosom of the lake,
And Arthur row'd across and took it –"

# THE DWARF

Now it is September and the web is woven.
The web is woven and you have to wear it.

The winter is made and you have to bear it,
The winter web, the winter woven, wind and wind,

For all the thoughts of summer that go with it
In the mind, pupa of straw, moppet of rags.

It is the mind that is woven, the mind that was jerked
And tufted in straggling thunder and shattered sun.

It is all that you are, the final dwarf of you,
That is woven and woven and waiting to be worn,

Neither as mask nor as garment but as a being,
Torn from insipid summer, for the mirror of cold,

Sitting beside your lamp, there citron to nibble
And coffee dribble . . . Frost is in the stubble.

# THE FAIRY

For Helen in virgin shadows and impassible radiance in the astral silence, ornamental saps conspired. Summer's ardour was confided to silent birds and indispensable indolence to a priceless mourning boat through gulfs of dead loves and fallen perfumes.

– After the moment of the woodswomen's song to the rumble of the torrent in the ruin of the wood, from the bells of the cattle to the echo of the vales, and the cries of the steppes. –

For Helen's childhood shadows and thickets shuddered, and the breast of the poor and the legends of the sky.

And her eyes and her dance superior, even to the precious glitterings, cold influences, or the pleasure of the unique setting and the unique hour.

TRANSLATED BY OLIVER BERNARD

# WILL O' THE WISP

This elfin sprite, as ancient legends say,
Was fairy-born; on him they did bestow
The art to lead poor villagers astray,
For an offence some thousand years ago.

This elfin sprite with meteor lantern hies
Close to the edge of slimy pool or lake;
Still like an anxious guide before them flies,
Nor, till some mischief done, does them forsake.

This elfin sprite have many tried to seize,
Yet in the rash attempt have suffered sore;
With mockery of himself he will them tease,
Which grasping hard, they see him still before.

Then on to fairy land, in gay despight,
Upon a zephyr will this elfin ride;
And all the fays do at his lantern light
Their little torches, and the feast provide.

Now seated round the tulip's ample bowl,
To jocund elves he doth his wiles betray;
In mirthful glee the hours unheeded roll,
Till dawn just peeps, then swift they hie away.

CHARLOTTE DACRE (1771 – 1825)

# THE SNOW FAIRY

## I

Throughout the afternoon I watched them there,
Snow-fairies falling, falling from the sky,
Whirling fantastic in the misty air,
Contending fierce for space supremacy.
And they flew down a mightier force at night,
As though in heaven there was revolt and riot,
And they, frail things had taken panic flight
Down to the calm earth seeking peace and quiet.
I went to bed and rose at early dawn
To see them huddled together in a heap,
Each merged into the other upon the lawn,
Worn out by the sharp struggle, fast asleep.
The sun shone brightly on them half the day,
By night they stealthily had stol'n away.

## II

And suddenly my thoughts then turned to you
Who came to me upon a winter's night,
When snow-sprites round my attic window flew,
Your hair disheveled, eyes aglow with light.
My heart was like the weather when you came,
The wanton winds were blowing loud and long;
But you, with joy and passion all aflame,
You danced and sang a lilting summer song.

I made room for you in my little bed,
Took covers from the closet fresh and warm,
A downful pillow for your scented head,
And lay down with you resting in my arm.
You went with Dawn. You left me ere the day,
The lonely actor of a dreamy play.

# FAIRY BEEKEEPER

You teach me patience, send jars of sunlight
that require careful straining. Your children

spin gold from acacia and rose, turn blood shades
into caring sweetness. You did not know me

from either inhabitant of Eden, but still you threw
wide your garden gates and said: *Come, taste.*

Whence I've come in such condition – my wings
in shreds, hum broken – you took the time to ask.

Now, I take my tea with a fine skim of wax.

# MERMAIDS AND WATER-FOLK

*Teach me to hear mermaids singing.*

JOHN DONNE (1572–1631), "Song: Go and Catch a Falling Star"

# THE SEA-FAIRIES

Slow sail'd the weary mariners and saw,
Betwixt the green brink and the running foam,
Sweet faces rounded arms, and bosoms prest
To little harps of gold; and while they mused
Whispering to each other half in fear,
Shrill music reach'd them on the middle sea.

Whither away, whither away, whither away? fly no
    more.
Whither away from the high green field, and the
    happy blossoming shore?
Day and night to the billow the fountain calls:
Down shower the gambolling waterfalls
From wandering over the lea:
Out of the live-green heart of the dells
They freshen the silvery-crimson shells,
And thick with white bells the clover-hill swells
High over the full-toned sea:
O hither, come hither and furl your sails,
Come hither to me and to me:
Hither, come hither and frolic and play;
Here it is only the mew that wails;
We will sing to you all the day:
Mariner, mariner, furl your sails,
For here are the blissful downs and dales,

And merrily, merrily carol the gales,
And the spangle dances in bight and bay,
And the rainbow forms and flies on the land
Over the islands free;
And the rainbow lives in the curve of the sand;
Hither, come hither and see;
And the rainbow hangs on the poising wave,
And sweet is the colour of cove and cave,
And sweet shall your welcome be:
O hither, come hither, and be our lords,
For merry brides are we:
We will kiss sweet kisses, and speak sweet words:
O listen, listen, your eyes shall glisten
With pleasure and love and jubilee:
O listen, listen, your eyes shall glisten
When the sharp clear twang of the golden chords
Runs up the ridged sea.
Who can light on as happy a shore
All the world o'er, all the world o'er?
Whither away? listen and stay: mariner, mariner, fly
    no more.

# THE LORELEY

I cannot tell why this imagined
  Despair has fallen on me;
The ghost of an ancient legend
  That will not let me be:

The air is cool, and twilight
  Flows down the quiet Rhine;
A mountain alone in the high light
  Still holds the faltering shine.

The last peak rosily gleaming
  Reveals, enthroned in air,
A maiden, lost in dreaming,
  Who combs her golden hair.

Combing her hair with a golden
  Comb in her rocky bower,
She sings the tune of an olden
  Song that has magical power.

The boatman has heard; it has bound him
  In throes of a strange, wild love;
Blind to the reefs that surround him,
  He sees but the vision above.

And lo, hungry waters are springing –
   Boat and boatman are gone. . . .
Then silence. And this, with her singing,
   The Loreley has done.

HEINRICH HEINE (1797 – 1856)
    TRANSLATED BY LOUIS UNTERMEYER

## LORELEI

It is no night to drown in:
A full moon, river lapsing
Black beneath bland mirror-sheen,

The blue water-mists dropping
Scrim after scrim like fishnets
Though fishermen are sleeping,

The massive castle turrets
Doubling themselves in a glass
All stillness. Yet these shapes float

Up toward me, troubling the face
Of quiet. From the nadir
They rise, their limbs ponderous

With richness, hair heavier
Than sculpted marble. They sing
Of a world more full and clear

Than can be. Sisters, your song
Bears a burden too weighty
For the whorled ear's listening

Here, in a well-steered country,
Under a balanced ruler.
Deranging by harmony

Beyond the mundane order,
Your voices lay siege. You lodge
On the pitched reefs of nightmare,

Promising sure harborage;
By day, descant from borders
Of hebetude, from the ledge

Also of high windows. Worse
Even than your maddening
Song, your silence. At the source

Of your ice-hearted calling –
Drunkenness of the great depths.
O river, I see drifting

Deep in your flux of silver
Those great goddesses of peace.
Stone, stone, ferry me down there.

# WATERMAID

Bright
with the armpit dazzle of a lioness
she answers,
wearing white light about her;
and the waves escort her,
my lioness,
crowned with moonlight.

So brief her presence –
match-flare in wind's breath –
so brief with mirrors around me.
Downward . . .
the waves distil her:
gold crop
sinking ungathered.

Watermaid of the salt-emptiness,
grown are the ears of the secret.

CHRISTOPHER OKIGBO (1932–67)                    79

## From THE LOVE SONG OF
## J. ALFRED PRUFROCK

I grow old . . . I grow old . . .
I shall wear the bottoms of my trousers rolled.

Shall I put my hair behind? Do I dare to eat a peach?
I shall wear white flannel trousers, and walk upon the
    beach.
I have heard the mermaids singing, each to each.

I do not think that they will sing to me.

I have seen them riding seaward on the waves
Combing the white hair of the waves blown back
When the wind blows the water white and black.

We have lingered in the chambers of the sea
By sea-girls wreathed with seaweed red and brown
Till human voices wake us, and we drown.

80    T. S. ELIOT (1888–1965)

# FABLE OF THE MERMAID
# AND THE DRUNKS

All these fellows were there inside
when she entered, utterly naked.
They had been drinking, and began to spit at her.
Recently come from the river, she understood nothing.
She was a mermaid who had lost her way.
The taunts flowed over her glistening flesh.
Obscenities drenched her golden breasts.
A stranger to tears, she did not weep.
A stranger to clothes, she did not dress.
They pocked her with cigarette ends and with burnt
    corks,
and rolled on the tavern floor in raucous laughter.
She did not speak, since speech was unknown to her.
Her eyes were the colour of faraway love,
her arms were matching topazes.
Her lips moved soundlessly in coral light,
and ultimately, she left by that door.
Hardly had she entered the river than she was
    cleansed,
gleaming once more like a white stone in the rain;
and without a backward look, she swam once more,
swam towards nothingness, swam to her dying.

PABLO NERUDA (1904–73)                    81
TRANSLATED BY ALASTAIR REID

## NÄCKEN (THE NIXIE)

Wreaths of golden cloud are glancing,
Elves upon the lea are dancing,
While the sedge-crowned nixie ever
Plays his fiddle from the river.

But a lad in clumps of willow,
Hearing music from the billow,
Calls o'er violet-perfumed meadows
Through the silent evening shadows:

"Poor old boy, how can you play so?
Can you make your sad heart gay so?
Though you cheer all else in nature,
You can never be God's creature.

"Heaven's beauteous moonlit bowers,
Eden crowned with blooming flowers,
Angels bright with hues elysian, –
These will never bless your vision."

Tears flow down the nixie's face then,
And he sinks to his own place then.
Silent is the fiddle. Never
Sounds the music from the river.

82   ERIK JOHAN STAGNELIUS (1810–40)
    TRANSLATED BY CHARLES WHARTON STORK

## RETURN TO MERMAID

I returned to her from overseas,
    unable to dunk away the desert
        sands and unwashable stains.
    She waited for me in the trailer
décor, a thrift-store museum
    of mismatched boat relics, walls
        lined with buoys, fish mounted
    on the walls with mouths agape,
posters of famous ocean tragedies.
    The carpeting was a polluted green
        sea and the overcast stucco ceiling
    a single cloud mass observing us.
My mermaid nested in the depth
    and depression of me, a glimpse
        of the man I drowned in fatigues.

## From A VISION OF THE MERMAIDS

Careless of me they sported: some would plash
The languent smooth with dimpling drops, and flash
Their filmy tails adown whose length there show'd
An azure ridge; or clouds of violet glow'd
On prankèd scale; or threads of carmine, shot
Thro' silver, gloom'd to a blood-vivid clot.
Some, diving merrily, downward drove, and gleam'd
With arm and fin; the argent bubbles stream'd
Airwards, disturb'd; and the scarce troubled sea
Gurgled, where they had sunk, melodiously.
Others with fingers white would comb among
The drenchèd hair of slabby weeds that swung
Swimming, and languish'd green upon the deep
Down that dank rock o'er which their lush long
     tresses weep.
  But most in a half-circle watch'd the sun;
And a sweet sadness dwelt on everyone;
I knew not why, – but know that sadness dwells
On Mermaids – whether that they ring the knells
Of seamen whelm'd in chasms of the mid-main,
As poets sing; or that it is a pain
To know the dusk depths of the ponderous sea,
The miles profound of solid green, and be
With loath'd cold fishes, far from man – or what; –
I know the sadness but the cause know not.

Then they, thus ranged, 'gan make full plaintively
A piteous Siren sweetness on the sea,
Withouten instrument, or conch, or bell,
Or stretch'd cords tuneable on turtle's shell;
Only with utterance of sweet breath they sung
An antique chaunt and in an unknown tongue.
Now melting upward thro' the sloping scale
Swell'd the sweet strain to a melodious wail;
Now ringing clarion-clear to whence it rose
Slumber'd at last in one sweet, deep, heart-broken
    close.
   But when the sun had lapsed to Ocean, lo
A stealthy wind crept round seeking to blow,
Linger'd, then raised the washing waves and drench'd
The floating blooms and with tide flowing quench'd
The rosy isles: so that I stole away
And gain'd thro' growing dusk the stirless bay;
White loom'd my rock, the water gurgling o'er,
Whence oft I watch but see those Mermaids now no
    more.

## LA SIRENA

I stalked her, for centuries.
My apologies.

From time to time, she crossed oceans,
found me, caressed me, tossed me with her
stoic palms, her rough scales stuffed
with the soliloquies of Argentine cinema
and roses.

Take my heart, I said. Take this oblong
jelly cave. The crosses? She asked, How
did you survive? *No me preguntes*, I told her.
Don't ask me. Ask me about this tortured sea,
your black tresses inside my eyes, infinite,
dying, blossoming.

# A SEA-SPELL

Her lute hangs shadowed in the apple-tree,
   While flashing fingers weave the sweet-strung spell
   Between its chords; and as the wild notes swell
The sea-bird for those branches leaves the sea.
But to what sound her listening ear stoops she?
   What nether world gulf-whispers doth she hear,
   In answering echoes from what planisphere,
Along the wind, along the estuary?

She sinks into her spell: and when full soon
   Her lips move and she soars unto her song,
   What creatures of the midmost main shall throng
In furrowed surf clouds to the summoning rune;
   Till he, the fated mariner, hears her cry,
   And up her rock, bare-breasted, comes to die!

## "NAIAD, WHOSE SLIDING LIPS WERE MINE"

Naiad, whose sliding lips were mine
No longer than the nightingale
Paused between one song and another,
Where sit you now the willow throws
Her last gold to the sullen river?

Do you among your sisters tell
Yet of a kiss so weighed with woe,
So mute, so cold, you doubt the giver
Still walks about the wintry earth,
But in some deep pool drowned soon after?

# QUEER FAIRIES

I want to be a mermaid, merman, *mermanmaid*.

TAYLOR MAC, *The Be(A)st of Taylor Mac* (2006)

*Let us gather therefore –*
*  in secure and consecrated places . . .*
*To re-invoke from ancient ashes our Fairy Circle . . .*

HARRY HAY (1980)

## THE IRIS WAS YELLOW,
## THE MOON WAS PALE

The iris was yellow, the moon was pale,
    In the air it was stiller than snow,
There was even light through the vale,
    But a vaporous sheet
    Clung about my feet,
  And I dared no further go.
I had passed the pond, I could see the stile,
The path was plain for more than a mile,
    Yet I dared no further go.

The iris-beds shone in my face, when, whist!
    A noiseless music began to blow,
A music that moved through the mist,
    That had not begun,
    That would never be done,
  With that music I must go:
And I found myself in the heart of the tune,
Wheeling round to the whirr of the moon,
    With the sheets of mist below.

In my hands how warm were the little hands,
   Strange, little hands that I did not know:
I did not think of the elvan bands,
     Nor of anything
     In that whirling ring –
   Here a cock began to crow!
The little hands dropped that had clung so tight,
And I saw again by the pale dawnlight
   The iris-heads in a row.

CAFÉ: 3 A.M.

Detectives from the vice squad
with weary sadistic eyes
spotting fairies.
> *Degenerates,*
> some folks say.

> But God, Nature,
> or somebody
> made them that way.

Police lady or Lesbian
over there?
> *Where?*

## TO O.E.A.

Your voice is the color of a robin's breast,
    And there's a sweet sob in it like rain – still rain in
        the night.
Among the leaves of the trumpet-tree, close to his
        nest,
    The pea-dove sings, and each note thrills me with
        strange delight
Like the words, wet with music, that well from your
        trembling throat.
    I'm afraid of your eyes, they're so bold,
    Searching me through, reading my thoughts,
        shining like gold.
But sometimes they are gentle and soft like the dew
        on the lips of the eucharis
Before the sun comes warm with his lover's kiss.
    You are sea-foam, pure with the star's loveliness,
Not mortal, a flower, a fairy, too fair for the beauty-
        shorn earth.
All wonderful things, all beautiful things, gave of
        their wealth to your birth.
Oh I love you so much, not recking of passion, that I
        feel it is wrong!
    But men will love you, flower, fairy, non-mortal
        spirit burdened with flesh,
Forever, life-long.

# TO CHARLES ON HIS HOME

Death is an unforgiven
That's what we have in common

language an act of sharing words.

Coming tears will do it

Where there's smoke
THERe's a suitcase

fairies never change

into fire

It's so hard to get to the top.

Death is a failure

there are so many of them.

Dont trust her
I don't care how old the races are.

And I never have.

for Cher.

JOHN WIENERS (1934–2002)                          95

## ONLY WHEN I

Only when I wing
am I dancing on the ground
Only when I fly
am I I
Only when I sing
am I quietly profound
Only when I glee
am I me

## RAINWATER FROM CERTAIN
## ENCHANTED STREAMS

After the foxes come, I wake, put on a self.
Sometimes still get *ma'am* on the phone (never *miss*).
Some friends call me fairy, dyke, & I'm all these
    things.
Cosmically I count seconds between my thighs (still
    thick)
and lightning. I inject, grow a beard, bleed awhile . . .
    I become my wildest self
through make-believe – to the river with this
    thunderous me: carrier and carried
both, everything else a tenderness held with string
    until it becomes my face entirely.
Me suckling through my own prow, family of foxes
    making yips & howls the others can hear
emanating from the woods.

From THE FAIRIES ARE DANCING ALL
OVER THE WORLD

... On sap green evenings in early summer
   the fairies danced under the moon in country
    places
 danced among native american teepees
and hung in the rough hair of buffalos racing across
  the prairies
    and are dancing still
    most hidden
    and everywhere
In some, only in the eyes
 in others a reach of the arm
  a sudden yelp of joy
reveals their presence
The fairies are dancing from coast to coast
 all over deadmiddle America
   they're bumping and grinding on the Kremlin
    walls
 the tap of their feet is eroding all the walls
  all over the world as they dance
In the way of the western world
  the fairies' dance has become small
 a bleating, crabbed jerkiness
but there for all that,
 a bit of healthy green in the dead wood

      that spreads an invisible green fire
  around and around the globe
encircling it in its dance
  of intimacy with the secret of all living things . . .

MICHAEL RUMAKER (1932–2019)       99

# FAIRY MUSIC
# AND DANCE

*"Over the hills and far away,"*
*That is the tune I heard one day.*
*Oh that I too might hear the cruel*
*Honey-sweet folk of the Hills of Ruel.*

FIONA MACLEOD (WILLIAM SHARPE),
"The Hills of Ruel" (1921)

## From A MIDSUMMER NIGHT'S DREAM

Over hil, over dale, through bush, through briar,
Over parke, over pale, through flood, through fire,
I do wander everie where, swifter then the Moons
    sphere;
And I serve the Fairy Queene, to dew her orbs upon
    the green.
The Cowslips tall, her pensioners bee,
In their gold coats, spots you see,
Those be Rubies, Fairie favors,
In those freckles, live their savors,
I must go seeke some dew drops here,
And hang a pearle in every cowslips eare.
Farewell thou Lob of spirits, Ile be gon,
Our Queene and all her Elves come heere anon.

## From THE TEMPEST

Where the bee sucks there suck I;
In a cowslip's bell I lie;
There I couch when owls do cry.
On the bat's back I do fly
After summer merrily.
Merrily, merrily shall I live now
Under the blossom that hangs on the bough.

WILLIAM SHAKESPEARE (1564–1616)

## From SONGS OF THE PIXIES

### I

Whom the untaught shepherds call
  Pixies in their madrigal,
Fancy's children, here we dwell:
  Welcome, ladies! to our cell.
Here the wren of softest note
  Builds its nest and warbles well;
Here the blackbird strains his throat;
  Welcome, ladies! to our cell.

### II

When fades the moon all shadowy-pale,
And scuds the cloud before the gale,
Ere morn with living gems bedight
Streaks the East with purple light,
We sip the furze flowers fragrant dews,
Clad in robes of rainbow hues
Richer than the deepened bloom
That glows on summer's scented plume:
Or sport amid the rosy gleam,
Soothed by the distant-tinkling team,
While lusty labour, scouting sorrow,
Bids the dame a glad good-morrow,
Who jogs th' accustomed road along,
And paces cheery to her cheering song.

## CUSHEEN LOO

Sleep, my child! for the rustling trees,
Stirr'd by the breath of summer breeze,
And fairy songs of sweetest note,
Around us gently float.

Sleep! for the weeping flowers have shed
Their fragrant tears upon thy head,
The voice of love hath sooth'd thy rest,
And thy pillow is a mother's breast.
                                    Sleep, my child!

Weary hath pass'd the time forlorn,
Since to your mansion I was borne,
Tho' bright the feast of its airy halls,
And the voice of mirth resounds from its walls.
                                    Sleep, my child!

Full many a maid and blooming bride
Within that splendid dome abide, –
And many a hoar and shrivell'd sage,
And many a matron bow'd with age.
                                    Sleep, my child!

Oh! thou who hearest this song of fear,
To the mourner's home these tidings bear.
Bid him bring the knife of the magic blade,
At whose lightning-flash the charm will fade.
                          Sleep, my child!

Haste! for to-morrow's sun will see
The hateful spell renewed for me;
Nor can I from that home depart,
Till life shall leave my withering heart.
                          Sleep, my child!

Sleep, my child! for the rustling trees,
Stirr'd by the breath of summer breeze,
And fairy songs of sweetest note,
Around us gently float.

# ELFENLIED (FAIRY SONG)

At midnight, when asleep are men at length,
Then shines for us the moon,
   Then gleams for us the star,
We rove and dance and sing,
   Nor gay till then we are.

At midnight, when asleep are men at length,
We seek the alder grove,
   And in the pale moonbeam,
We rove about and sing,
   And gaily dance a dream.

JOHANN WOLFGANG VON GOETHE (1749–1832)    107
TRANSLATED BY WILLIAM GRASETT THOMAS

# ELFENLIED (FAIRY SONG)

At night in the village the watchman shouted
                    "Elf!"
A tiny little elf was asleep in the wood –
                    Just around eleven;
And he thinks that from the dale
He was called by his name by the nightingale,
Or that Silpelit might have called him.
So the elf rubs his eyes,
Steps out before his snail-shell house,
And is much like a drunken man,
His sleep not fully completed;
And he hobbles thusly, tippy-tap,
Through the hazel wood down to the dale,
Slips along the vineyard wall,
On which many fireflies are glowing.
"What are those bright windows?
There must be a wedding inside;
The little people are sitting at the feast,
And make merry in the hall.
So I'll just take a peep inside!"
– Fie! he hits his head on hard stone!
Well, elf, had enough, have you?
                    Cuckoo! Cuckoo!

EDUARD MÖRIKE (1804–75)
        TRANSLATED BY WERNER SINGER

# DONG, SOUNDS THE BRASS IN THE EAST

Dong, sounds the brass in the east,
As if to a funeral feast,
But I like that sound the best
Out of the fluttering west

The steeple ringeth a knell,
But the fairies' silvery bell
Is the voice of that gentle folk,
Or else the horizon that spoke

Its metal is not of brass,
But air, and water, and glass,
And under a cloud it is swung,
And by the wind it is rung

When the steeple tolleth the noon,
It soundeth not so soon,
Yet it rings a far earlier hour,
And the sun has not reached its tower

HENRY DAVID THOREAU (1817–62)

# THE FAIRY FIDDLER

'Tis I go fiddling, fiddling,
By weedy ways forlorn;
I make the blackbird's music
Ere in his breast 'tis born:
The sleeping larks I waken
'Twixt the midnight and the morn.

No man alive has seen me,
But women hear me play
Sometimes at door or window,
Fiddling the souls away, –
The child's soul and the colleen's
Out of the covering clay.

None of my fairy kinsmen
Makes music with me now:
Alone the raths I wander
Or ride the whitethorn bough,
But the wild swans they know me
And the horse that draws the plough.

## THE CORN-STALK FIDDLE

When the corn's all cut and the bright stalks shine
    Like the burnished spears of a field of gold;
When the field-mice rich on the nubbins dine,
    And the frost comes white and the wind blows cold;
Then its heigho fellows and hi-diddle-diddle,
For the time is ripe for the corn-stalk fiddle.

And you take a stalk that is straight and long,
    With an expert eye to its worthy points,
And you think of the bubbling strains of song
    That are bound between its pithy joints –
Then you cut out strings, with a bridge in the middle,
With a corn-stalk bow for a corn-stalk fiddle.

Then the strains that grow as you draw the bow
    O'er the yielding strings with a practiced hand!
And the music's flow never loud but low
    Is the concert note of a fairy band.
Oh, your dainty songs are a misty riddle
To the simple sweets of the corn-stalk fiddle.

When the eve comes on and our work is done
    And the sun drops down with a tender glance,
With their hearts all prime for the harmless fun,
    Come the neighbor girls for the evening's dance,

And they wait for the well-known twist and twiddle,
More time than tune – from the corn-stalk fiddle.

Then brother Jabez takes the bow,
    While Ned stands off with Susan Bland,
Then Henry stops by Milly Snow
    And John takes Nellie Jones's hand.
While I pair off with Mandy Biddle,
And scrape, scrape, scrape goes the corn-stalk fiddle.

"Salute your partners," comes the call,
    "All join hands and circle round,"
"Grand train back," and "Balance all,"
    Footsteps lightly spurn the ground,
"Take your lady and balance down the middle"
To the merry strains of the corn-stalk fiddle.

So the night goes on and the dance is o'er,
    And the merry girls are homeward gone,
But I see it all in my sleep once more,
    And I dream till the very break of dawn
Of an impish dance on a red-hot griddle
To the screech and scrape of a corn-stalk fiddle.

# LYRICS TO THE TUNE "FAIRY GROTTO"

Skin of ice.
Bones of jade.
Always cool and unperspiring.

To the palace by the water
Comes a breeze,
Filling it with hidden fragrance.

Embroidered curtains open.
A ray of moonlight
Peeks in at her.
She is not yet asleep.
But leans against the pillow,
Hairpin awry
And hair tousled.

She rises.
I take her white hand.
In all the doors and courtyards
There is silence.
From time to time
A shooting star
Crosses the Milky Way.

I ask how late it is:
Already midnight.
Golden waves of moonlight fade,
The stars of the Jeweled Cord
Roll low.

On my fingers I count the time
Until the west wind comes again,
Saying nothing of the flowing years
That steal away in darkness.

114   SU SHE (1037 – 1101)
        TRANSLATED BY GREG WHINCUP

## From THE ROMANCE OF THE FOREST

AIR

Now, at Moonlight's fairy hour,
    When faintly gleams each dewy steep,
And vale and Mountain, lake and bow'r,
    In solitary grandeur sleep;

When slowly sinks the evening breeze,
    That lulls the mind in pensive care,
And Fancy loftier visions sees,
    Bid Music wake the silent air.

Bid the merry, merry tabor sound,
    And with the Fays of lawn or glade,
In tripping circlet beat the ground,
    Under the high trees' trembling shade.

"Now, at Moonlight's fairy hour,"
    Shall Music breathe her dulcet voice,
And o'er the waves, with magic pow'r,
    Call on Echo to rejoice.

ANN RADCLIFFE (1764–1823)                    115

## From A MASQUE PRESENTED AT LUDLOW CASTLE

Mean while welcom Joy, and Feast,
Midnight shout, and revelry,
Tipsie dance and Jollity.
Braid your Locks with rosie Twine
Dropping odours, dropping Wine.
Rigor now is gone to bed,
And Advice with scrupulous head,
Strict Age, and sowre Severity,
With their grave Saws in slumber ly.
We that are of purer fire
Imitate the Starry Quire,
Who in their nightly watchfull Sphears,
Lead in swift round the Months and Years.
The Sounds, and Seas with all their finny drove
Now to the Moon in wavering Morrice move,
And on the Tawny Sands and Shelves,
Trip the pert Fairies and the dapper Elves;
By dimpled Brook, and Fountain brim,
The Wood-Nymphs deckt with Daisies trim,
Their merry wakes and pastimes keep:
What hath night to do with sleep?
Night hath better sweets to prove,
Venus now wakes, and wak'ns Love.

Cum let us our rights begin,
Tis onely day-light that makes Sin,
Which these dun shades will ne're report.

# THE FAËRY CHASM

No fiction was it of the antique age:
A sky-blue stone, within this sunless cleft,
Is of the very foot-marks unbereft
Which tiny Elves impressed; – on that smooth stage

Dancing with all their brilliant equipage
In secret revels – haply after theft
Of some sweet Babe – Flower stolen, and coarse
  Weed left
For the distracted Mother to assuage
Her grief with, as she might! – But, where, oh! where

Is traceable a vestige of the notes
That ruled those dances wild in character? –
Deep underground? Or in the upper air,
On the shrill wind of midnight? or where floats
O'er twilight fields the autumnal gossamer?

# FAËRY MORRIS

The winds are whist; and, hid in mist,
The moon hangs o'er the wooded height;
The bushy bee, with unkempt head,
Hath made the sunflower's disk his bed,
    And sleeps half-hid from sight.
    The owlet makes us melody –
    Come dance with us in Faëry,
      Come dance with us to-night.

The dew is damp; the glow-worm's lamp
Blurs in the moss its tawny light;
The great gray moth sinks, half-asleep,
Where, in an elfin-laundered heap,
    The lily-gowns hang white.
    The crickets make us minstrelsy –
    Come dance with us in Faëry,
      Come dance with us to-night.

With scents of heat, dew-chilled and sweet,
The new-cut hay smells by the bight;
The ghost of some dead pansy bloom,
The butterfly dreams in the gloom,
    Its pied wings folded tight.
    The world is lost in fantasy, –
    Come dance with us in Faëry,
      Come dance with us to-night.

MADISON JULIUS CAWEIN (1865 – 1914)        119

## From THE FAIRIES FEGARIES

Come follow, follow me,
You Fairie Elves that be:
And circle round this greene,
Come follow me your Queene.
Hand in hand lets dance a round,
For this place is Fayrie ground.

When Mortals are at rest,
And snorting in their nest,
Unheard, or unespy'd
Through key-holes we do glide:
Over tables, stooles and shelves,
We trip it with our Fairie Elves.

And if the house be foule,
Or platter, dish, or bowle,
Up stairs we nimbly creepe,
And finde the sluts asleepe:
Then we pinch their armes and thighes,
None escapes, nor none espies.

But if the house be swept,
And from uncleannesse kept,
We praise the house and maid,
And surely she is paid:

For we do use before we go
To drop a Tester in her shoe.

Upon the mushroomes head,
Our table cloth we spread
A graine o' th' finest wheat
Is manchet that we eate:
The pearlie drops of dew we drinke
In Akorne-cups fill'd to the brinke.

The tongues of Nightingales,
With unctuous iuyce of Snailes,
Betwixt two nut-shels stewde
Is meat thats easily chewde:
The braines of Rennes, the beards of mice
Will make a feast of wondrous price.

Over the tender grasse,
So lightly we can passe,
The yong and tender stalke,
Nere bowes whereon we walke,
Nor in the morning dew is seene,
Over night where we have beene.

The grass-hopper, gnat and flie,
Serves for our Minstrels three,
And sweetly dance a while,
Till we the time beguile:
And when the Moone-calfe hides her head,
The glow-worme lights us unto bed.

# FAIRIES

Maiden-Poet, come with me
To the heaped up cairn of Maeve,
And there we'll dance a fairy dance
Upon a fairy's grave.

In and out among the trees,
Filling all the night with sound,
The morning, strung upon her star,
Shall chase us round and round.

What are we but fairies too,
Living but in dreams alone,
Or, at the most, but children still,
Innocent and overgrown?

FRANCIS LEDWIDGE (1887 – 1917)

# THE FAIRY DANCE

The fairies are dancing – how nimbly they bound!
They flit o'er the grass tops, they touch not the ground;
Their kirtles of green are with diamonds bedight,
All glittering and sparkling beneath the moonlight.

Hark, hark to their music! how silvery and clear –
'Tis surely the flower-bells that ringing I hear, –
The lazy-wing'd moth, with the grasshopper wakes,
And the field-mouse peeps out, and their revels partakes.

How featly they trip it! how happy are they
Who pass all their moments in frolic and play,
Who rove where they list, without sorrows or cares,
And laugh at the fetters mortality wears!

But where have they vanish'd? – a cloud's o'er the moon,
I'll hie to the spot, – they'll be seen again soon –
I hasten – 'tis lighter, – and what do I view? –
The fairies were grasses, the diamonds were dew.

And thus do the sparkling illusions of youth
Deceive and allure, and we take them for truth;
Too happy are they who the juggle unshroud,
Ere the hint to inspect them be brought by a cloud.

# THE FAERY REEL

If I were young as once I was,
    and dreams and death more distant then,
I wouldn't split my soul in two,
    and keep half in the world of men,
So half of me would stay at home,
    and strive for Faërie in vain,
While all the while my soul would stroll
    up narrow path, down crooked lane,
And there would meet a faery lass
    and smile and bow with kisses three,
She'd pluck wild eagles from the air
    and nail me to a lightning tree
And if my heart would run from her
    or flee from her, be gone from her,
She'd wrap it in a nest of stars
    and then she'd take it on with her
Until one day she'd tire of it,
    all bored with it and done with it.

She'd leave it by a burning brook,
    and off brown boys would run with it.
They'd take it and have fun with it
    and stretch it long and cruel and thin,
They'd slice it into four and then
    they'd string with it a violin.

And every day and every night
   they'd play upon my heart a song
So plaintive and so wild and strange
   that all who heard it danced along
And sang and whirled and sank and trod
   and skipped and slipped and reeled and rolled
Until, with eyes as bright as coals,
   they'd crumble into wheels of gold. . . .

But I am young no longer now,
   for sixty years my heart's been gone
To play its dreadful music there,
   beyond the valley of the sun.
I watch with envious eyes and mind,
   the single-souled, who dare not feel
The wind that blows beyond the moon,
   who do not hear the Faery Reel.
If you don't hear the Faery Reel,
   they will not pause to steal your breath.
When I was young I was a fool.
   So wrap me up in dreams and death.

# FAIRY MISCHIEF
# AND MALEVOLENCE

*From fairies and the tempters of the night*
*Guard me!*

WILLIAM SHAKESPEARE, *Cymbeline* (1611)

# THE FAYRIES' DAUNCE

Dare you haunt our hallowed green?
None but fayries here are seene.
     Downe and sleepe,
     Wake and weepe,
Pinch him black, and pinch him blew,
That seekes to steale a lover true.
When you come to heare us sing,
Or to tread our fayrie ring,
Pinch him black, and pinch him blew,
O thus our nayles shall handle you.

THOMAS RAVENSCROFT (1582 – 1635)

## SONG OF FAIRIES ROBBING ORCHARD
From *Randolph*

We the Fairies, blithe and antic,
Of dimensions not gigantic,
Though the moonshine mostly keep us
Oft in orchards frisk and peep us.

Stolen sweets are always sweeter,
Stolen kisses much completer,
Stolen looks are nice in chapels,
Stolen, stolen be your apples.

When to bed the world are bobbing,
Then's the time for orchard robbing;
Yet the fruit were scarce worth peeling
Were it not for stealing, stealing.

## From THE MAD-MERRY PRANKES OF ROBBIN GOOD-FELLOW

From *Oberon* in Fairy Land,
  the King of Ghosts and shadowes there,
Mad *Robbin* I at his command,
  am sent to view the night-sports here
        What revell rout
        Is kept about
In every corner where I goe
        I will ore see,
        And merry be,
And make good sport with ho ho ho.

More swift than lightening can I flye,
  and round about this ayrie welkin soone,
And in a minutes space descry
  each thing that's done the Moone:
        There's not a Hag
        Nor Ghost shall wag,
Nor cry Goblin where I do goe,
        But *Robbin* I
        Their seats will spye
And feare them home with ho ho ho.

If any wanderers I meet
   that from their night sports doe trudge home,
With counterfeiting voyce I greet,
   and cause them on with me to roame
         Through woods, through lakes,
         Through bogs, through brakes,
Ore bush and brier with them I goe,
         I call upon
         Them to come on,
And wend me laughing ho, ho, ho.

Sometimes I meet them like a man,
   sometimes an oxe, sometimes a hound,
And to a horse I turne me can,
   to trip and trot about them round,
         But if to ride
         My backe they stride,
More swift than winde away I goe,
         Ore hedge and lands,
         Through pooles and ponds,
I whirry laughing ho, ho, ho.

When Ladds and Lasses merry be,
　With possets and with junkets fine,
Unseene of all the Company,
　I eate their cates and sip their wine:
　　　　and to make sport,
　　　　I fart and snort,
And out the candles I' doe blow,
　　　　The maids I kisse,
　　　　They shrieke who's this,
I answer nought but ho, ho, ho.

Yet now and then the maids to please,
　I card at midnight up their wooll:
And while they sleep, snort, fart, and fease,
　with wheele to threds their flaxe I pull:
　　　　I grind at Mill
　　　　Their Malt up still,
I dress their hemp, I spin their towe –
　　　　If any wake
　　　　And would me take,
I wend me laughing ho, ho, ho.

# THE FAIRIES

Up the airy mountain,
  Down the rushy glen,
We daren't go a-hunting
  For fear of little men;
Wee folk, good folk,
  Trooping all together;
Green jacket, red cap,
  And white owl's feather!

Down along the rocky shore
  Some make their home,
They live on crispy pancakes
  Of yellow tide-foam;
Some in the reeds
  Of the black mountain lake,
With frogs for their watch-dogs,
  All night awake.

High on the hill-top
  The old King sits;
He is now so old and gray
  He's nigh lost his wits.
With a bridge of white mist
  Columbkill he crosses,

On his stately journeys
  From Slieveleague to Rosses;
Or going up with the music
  On cold starry nights,
To sup with the Queen
  Of the gay Northern Lights.

They stole little Bridget
  For seven years long;
When she came down again
  Her friends were all gone.
They took her lightly back,
  Between the night and morrow,
They thought that she was fast asleep,
  But she was dead with sorrow.
They have kept her ever since
  Deep within the lake,
On a bed of flag-leaves,
  Watching till she wake.

By the craggy hill-side,
  Through the mosses bare,
They have planted thorn-trees
  For pleasure here and there.
Is any man so daring
  As dig up them in spite,

He shall find their sharpest thorns
   In his bed at night.

Up the airy mountain,
   Down the rushy glen,
We daren't go a-hunting
   For fear of little men;
Wee folk, good folk,
   Trooping all together;
Green jacket, red cap,
   And white owl's feather!

# PIXIE-LED

A breath on my forehead
   A laugh in my ear,
A shrill sound of fairy pipes
   Blowing near and clear;
Away from home and kindred,
   And out of street and town,
I wandered with the fairy folk
   Towards the mountain brown.
They led me thro' the live-long day,
   By field and moorland wide,
With a pattering of wee feet
   Running close beside;
And when I thought I saw them,
   O nothing could I find,
Only a dry leaf on the road
   Dancing in the wind.
The light was dead suddenly,
   And hills shut me in:
The curlews cried in the grey dusk,
   Across the gorse and whin,
Between the wild waste of the moor
   And the great lonely sky,
And the stream upon its cold stones
   Sobbing wearily.

CICELY FOX SMITH (1882–1954)

## From GOBLIN MARKET

Laughed every goblin
When they spied her peeping:
Came towards her hobbling,
Flying, running, leaping,
Puffing and blowing,
Chuckling, clapping, crowing,
Clucking and gobbling,
Mopping and mowing,
Full of airs and graces,
Pulling wry faces,
Demure grimaces,
Cat-like and rat-like,
Ratel- and wombat-like,
Snail-paced in a hurry,
Parrot-voiced and whistler,
Helter skelter, hurry skurry,
Chattering like magpies,
Fluttering like pigeons,
Gliding like fishes, –
Hugged her and kissed her:
Squeezed and caressed her:
Stretched up their dishes,
Panniers and plates:
"Look at our apples
Russet and dun,

Bob at our cherries
Bite at our peaches,
Citrons and dates,
Grapes for the asking,
Pears red with basking
Out in the sun,
Plums on their twigs;
Pluck them and suck them, –
Pomegranates, figs."

CHRISTINA ROSSETTI (1830–94)

# ERKLÖNIG (THE ERL-KING)

Who rideth so late through the night-wind wild?
It is the father with his child;
He has the little one well in his arm;
He holds him safe, and he folds him warm.

My son, why hidest thy face so shy? –
Seest thou not, father, the Erl-king nigh?
The Erlen king, with train and crown? –
It is a wreath of mist, my son.

"Come, lovely boy, come, go with me;
Such merry plays I will play with thee;
Many a bright flower grows on the strand,
And my mother has many a gay garment at hand."

My father, my father, dost thou not hear
What the Erl-king whispers low in my ear? –
Be quiet, my darling, be quiet, my child;
Through withered leaves the wind howls wild.

"Come, lovely boy, wilt thou go with me?
My daughters fair shall wait on thee;
My daughters their nightly revels keep;
They'll sing, and they'll dance, and they'll rock thee
        to sleep."

My father, my father, and seest thou not
The Erl-King's daughters in yon dim spot? –
My son, my son, I see and I know
'T is the old gray willow that shimmers so.

"I love thee, I dote on thy face so divine,
And art thou not willing, then force makes thee
      mine."
O father, the Erl-king now puts forth his arm!
O father, the Erl-king has done me harm!

The father shudders; he hurries on;
And faster he holds his moaning son;
He reaches his home with fear and dread,
And, lo! in his arms the child was dead!

JOHANN WOLFGANG VON GOETHE (1749–1832)    141
TRANSLATED BY F. H. HEDGE

## From TRISTRAM AND ISEULT

Merlin and Vivian stopp'd on the slope's brow
To gaze on the green sea of leaf and bough
Which glistering lay all round them, lone and mild,
As if to itself the quiet forest smil'd.
Upon the brow-top grew a thorn; and here
The grass was dry and moss'd, and you saw clear
Across the hollow: white anemonies
Starr'd the cool turf, and clumps of primroses
Ran out from the dark underwood behind.
No fairer resting-place a man could find.
"Here let us halt," said Merlin then; and she
Nodded, and tied her palfrey to a tree.

They sate them down together, and a sleep
Fell upon Merlin, more like death, so deep.
Her finger on her lips, then Vivian rose,
And from her brown-lock'd head the wimple throws,
And takes it in her hand, and waves it over
The blossom'd thorn-tree and her sleeping lover.
Nine times she wav'd the fluttering wimple round,
And made a little plot of magic ground.
And in that daisied circle, as men say,
Is Merlin prisoner till the judgement-day,
But she herself whither she will can rove,
For she was passing weary of his love.

## SWEDISH BALLAD: SIR OLOF
## AND THE FAIRIES

Sir Olof he rode out at early day,
And so came he unto an Elve-dance gay.
      The dance it goes well,
      So well in the grove.

The Elve-father reached out his white hand free,
"Come, come, Sir Olof, tread the dance with me."
      The dance it goes well,
      So well in the grove.

"O nought I will, and nought I may,
To-morrow will be my wedding-day."
      The dance it goes well,
      So well in the grove.

And the bride she spake with her bride-maids so,
"What may it mean that the bells thus go?"
      The dance it goes well,
      So well in the grove.

"'Tis the custom of this our isle," they replied;
"Each young swain ringeth home his bride."
      The dance it goes well,
      So well in the grove.

"And the truth from you to conceal I fear,
Sir Olof is dead, and lies on his bier."
      The dance it goes well,
       So well in the grove.

And on the morrow, ere light was the day,
In Sir Olof's house three corpses lay.
      The dance it goes well,
       So well in the grove.

It was Sir Olof, his bonny bride,
And eke his mother, of sorrow she died.
      The dance it goes well,
       So well in the grove.

144  ANONYMOUS (*c.* 14TH–15TH CENTURY)
TRANSLATED BY THOMAS KEIGHTLEY

# SEDUCTIONS AND ABDUCTIONS

*The fairies, the fairies, the mischief-loving fairies,*
  *Have stolen my loved one, my darling, and my dear;*
*With charms and enchantments they lured and waylaid him,*
*So my love cannot comfort and my presence cannot cheer.*

DORA SIGERSON SHORTER, "The Fairies" (1897)

# LA BELLE DAME SANS MERCI: A BALLAD

O what can ail thee, knight at arms,
  Alone and palely loitering?
The sedge has wither'd from the lake,
    And no birds sing.

O what can ail thee, knight at arms,
  So haggard and so woe-begone?
The squirrel's granary is full,
    And the harvest's done.

I see a lily on thy brow
  With anguish moist and fever dew,
And on thy cheeks a fading rose
    Fast withereth too.

I met a lady in the meads,
  Full beautiful, a fairy's child;
Her hair was long, her foot was light,
    And her eyes were wild.

I made a garland for her head,
  And bracelets too, and fragrant zone;
She look'd at me as she did love,
    And made sweet moan.

I set her on my pacing steed,
    And nothing else saw all day long,
For sidelong would she bend, and sing
        A fairy's song.

She found me roots of relish sweet,
    And honey wild, and manna dew,
And sure in language strange she said –
        I love thee true.

She took me to her elfin grot,
    And there she wept, and sigh'd full sore,
And there I shut her wild wild eyes
        With kisses four.

And there she lulled me asleep,
    And there I dream'd – Ah! woe betide!
The latest dream I ever dream'd
        On the cold hill's side.

I saw pale kings, and princes too,
    Pale warriors, death pale were they all;
They cried – "La belle dame sans merci
        Hath thee in thrall!"

I saw their starv'd lips in the gloam
  With horrid warning gaped wide,
And I awoke and found me here
    On the cold hill's side.

And this is why I sojourn here,
  Alone and palely loitering
Though the sedge is wither'd from the lake,
    And no birds sing.

## From SIR LAUNFAL

And she, advancing through the palace hall –
No fairer creature ever entered there –
Stepped from her horse before the King, and stood
Where all might look upon her. Then, when all
Had looked, and in their eyes she read their praise
And knew their hearts were won, she spake and said:
"Arthur, give ear. And give ye ear who make
King Arthur's court. I whom ye look upon
Once loved Sir Launfal. He before this court
Hath been accused of crime against the Queen. –
The Queen hath lied! He loveth me too dear
For other love. – As for his boast, my lords,
It is not I, but ye, should make award
Whether through me he be acquit thereof."
She spake, and all with one accord adjudge
That Launfal be exonerate from blame. –
Nor doth the King gainsay the just decree.

Then straight – without a word or glance for him
She came to save – she leaped where stood her steed,
And though the King and all his knights essayed
To hinder her, entreating her to stay,
Heeded them not, but like a lightning-flash
Galloped amid the throng, and through the portal. –
But Launfal, with the swiftness of sharp fear

Lest he should lose her alway, ran where rose
Without the palace gateway an old stone,
Whence Arthur's heavy-armored knights were wont
To mount their steeds. Thence sprang he, with mad
    leap,
Upon his lady's palfrey as she fled
From out the palace, and the hurrying steed
Carried the twain away to fairyworld,
To wondrous Avalon – so the Bretons sing –
And nevermore was Launfal seen of men.

MARIE DE FRANCE (1160–1215)      151
TRANSLATED BY FREDERICK BLISS LUQUIENS

# THE SONG OF WANDERING AENGUS

I went out to the hazel wood,
Because a fire was in my head,
And cut and peeled a hazel wand,
And hooked a berry to a thread;
And when white moths were on the wing,
And moth-like stars were flickering out,
I dropped the berry in a stream
And caught a little silver trout.

When I had laid it on the floor
I went to blow the fire aflame,
But something rustled on the floor,
And some one called me by my name:
It had become a glimmering girl
With apple blossom in her hair
Who called me by my name and ran
And faded through the brightening air.

Though I am old with wandering
Through hollow lands and hilly lands,
I will find out where she has gone,
And kiss her lips and take her hands;
And walk among long dappled grass,
And pluck till time and times are done
The silver apples of the moon,
The golden apples of the sun.

# HAPPY, HAPPY IT IS TO BE

"Happy, happy it is to be
Where the greenwood hangs o'er the dark blue sea;
To roam in the moonbeams clear and still
And dance with the elves
Over dale and hill;
To taste their cups, and with them roam
The field for dewdrops and honeycomb.
Climb then, and come, as quick as you can,
And dwell with the fairies, Elizabeth Ann!

"Never, never, comes tear or sorrow,
In the mansions old where the fairies dwell;
But only the harping of their sweet harp-strings,
And the lonesome stroke of a distant bell,
Where upon hills of thyme and heather,
The shepherd sits with his wandering sheep;
And the curlew wails, and the skylark hovers
Over the sand where the conies creep;
Climb then, and come, as quick as you can,
And dwell with the fairies, Elizabeth Ann!"

WALTER DE LA MARE (1873 – 1956)

# THE FAIRY LOVER

It was by yonder thorn I saw the fairy host
(O low night wind, O wind of the west!)
My love rode by, there was gold upon his brow,
And since that day I can neither eat nor rest.

I dare not pray lest I should forget his face
(O black north wind blowing cold beneath the sky!)
His face and his eyes shine between me and the sun:
If I may not be with him I would rather die.

They tell me I am cursed and I will lose my soul,
(O red wind shrieking o'er the thorn-grown dún!)
But he is my love and I go to him to-night,
Who rides when the thorn glistens white beneath
        the moon.

He will call my name and lift me to his breast,
(Blow soft O wind 'neath the stars of the south!)
I care not for heaven and I fear not hell
If I have but the kisses of his proud red mouth.

154   MOIREEN FOX CHEAVASA (1883–1972)

# THE LOVE-TALKER

I know not what way he came, no shadow fell behind,
But all the sighing rushes swayed beneath a fairy
     wind:
The thrush ceased its singing, a mist crept about,
We two clung together – with the world shut out.

Beyond the ghostly mist I could hear my cattle low,
The little cow from Ballina, clean as driven snow,
The dun cow from Kerry, the roan from Inisheer,
Oh, pitiful their calling – and his whispers in my ear!

His eyes were a fire; his words were a snare;
I cried my mother's name, but no help was there;
I made the blessed Sign: then he gave a dreary moan,
A wisp of cloud went floating by, and I stood alone.

ETHNA CARBERY (1866–1902)                                    155

# THE WIND ON THE HILLS

Go not to the hills of Erinn
When the night winds are about,
Put up your bar and shutter,
And so keep the danger out.

For the good-folk whirl within it,
And they pull you by the hand,
And they push you on the shoulder,
Till you move to their command.

And lo! you have forgotten
What you have known of tears,
And you will not remember
That the world goes full of years;

A year there is a lifetime,
And a second but a day,
And an older world will meet you
Each morn you come away.

Your wife grows old with weeping,
And your children one by one
Grow grey with nights of watching,
Before your dance is done.

And it will chance some morning
You will come home no more;
Your wife sees but a withered leaf
In the wind about the door.

And your children will inherit
The unrest of the wind,
They shall seek some face elusive,
And some land they never find.

When the wind is loud, they sighing
Go with hearts unsatisfied,
For some joy beyond remembrance,
For some memory denied.

And all your children's children,
They cannot sleep or rest,
When the wind is out in Erinn
And the sun is in the West.

DORA SIGERSON SHORTER (1866–1918)

# THE HAUNTED SPRING

Gaily through the mountain glen
   The hunter's horn did ring,
      As the milk-white doe
      Escaped his bow,
   Down by the haunted spring.
In vain his silver horn he wound, —
   'Twas echo answered back;
For neither groom nor baying hound
   Were on the hunter's track;
In vain he sought the milk-white doe
That made him stray, and 'scaped his bow;
For, save himself, no living thing
Was by the silent haunted spring.

The purple heath-bells, blooming fair,
   Their fragrance round did fling,
      As the hunter lay
      At close of day,
   Down by the haunted spring.
A lady fair, in robe of white,
   To greet the hunter came;
She kissed a cup with jewels bright,
   And pledged him by his name;
"Oh, lady fair," the hunter cried,
"Be thou my love, my blooming bride,

A bride that well may grace a king!
Fair lady of the haunted spring."

In the fountain clear she stoop'd,
   And forth she drew a ring;
        And that loved Knight
        His faith did plight
   Down by the haunted spring.
But since that day his chase did stray,
   The hunter ne'er was seen,
And legends tell, he now doth dwell
   Within the hills so green;
But still the milk-white doe appears,
And wakes the peasants' evening fears,
While distant bugles faintly ring
Around the lonely haunted spring.

SAMUEL LOVER (1797 – 1868)                    159

# THE FAIRY THRALL

On gossamer nights when the moon is low,
  And the stars in the mist are hiding,
Over the hill where the foxgloves grow
  You may see the fairies riding.
      Kling! klang! kling!
      Their stirrups and their bridles ring,
    And their horns are loud and their bugles blow,
    When the moon is low.

They sweep through the night like a whistling wind,
  They pass and have left no traces;
But one of them lingers far behind
  The flight of the fairy faces.
      She makes moan,
      She sorrows in the dark alone,
    She wails for the love of human kind,
    Like a whistling wind.

"Ah! why did I roam where the elfins ride,
  Their glimmering steps to follow?
They bore me far from my loved one's side,
  To wander o'er hill and hollow.
      Kling! klang! kling!
      Their stirrups and their bridles ring,
    But my heart is cold in the cold night-tide,
    Where the elfins ride."

160   MARY C. G. BYRON (1861–1936)

# THE STOLEN CHILD

Where dips the rocky highland
Of Sleuth Wood in the lake,
There lies a leafy island
Where flapping herons wake
The drowsy water-rats;
There we've hid our faery vats,
Full of berries
And of reddest stolen cherries.
*Come away, O human child!*
*To the waters and the wild*
*With a faery, hand in hand,*
*For the world's more full of weeping than you can*
*understand.*

Where the wave of moonlight glosses
The dim grey sands with light,
Far off by furthest Rosses
We foot it all the night,
Weaving olden dances,
Mingling hands and mingling glances
Till the moon has taken flight;
To and fro we leap
And chase the frothy bubbles,
While the world is full of troubles
And is anxious in its sleep.

*Come away, O human child!*
*To the waters and the wild*
*With a faery, hand in hand,*
*For the world's more full of weeping than you can*
    *understand.*

Where the wandering water gushes
From the hills above Glen-Car,
In pools among the rushes
That scarce could bathe a star,
We seek for slumbering trout
And whispering in their ears
Give them unquiet dreams;
Leaning softly out
From ferns that drop their tears
Over the young streams.
*Come away, O human child!*
*To the waters and the wild*
*With a faery, hand in hand,*
*For the world's more full of weeping than you can*
    *understand.*

Away with us he's going,
The solemn-eyed:
He'll hear no more the lowing
Of the calves on the warm hillside
Or the kettle on the hob

Sing peace into his breast,
Or see the brown mice bob
Round and round the oatmeal-chest.
*For he comes, the human child,*
*To the waters and the wild*
*With a faery, hand in hand,*
*From a world more full of weeping than he can*
*understand.*

# THE FAIRY CHILD

The summer sun was sinking
   With a mild light, calm and mellow;
It shone on my little boy's bonnie cheeks,
   And his loose locks of yellow.

The robin was singing sweetly,
   And his song was sad and tender,
And my little boy's eyes, while he heard the song,
   Smiled with a sweet, soft splendor.

My little boy lay on my bosom
   While his soul the song was quaffing;
The joy of his soul had tinged his cheek,
   And his heart and his eye were laughing.

I sate alone in my cottage,
   The midnight needle plying;
I feared for my child, for the rush's light
   In the socket now was dying;

Then came a hand to my lonely latch,
   Like the wind at midnight moaning;
I knelt to pray, but rose again
   For I heard my little boy groaning.

I crossed my brow and I crossed my breast,
   But that night my child departed, –
They left a weakling in his stead,
   And I am broken-hearted!

O, it cannot be my own sweet boy,
   For his eyes are dim and hollow,
My little boy is gone – is gone,
   And his mother soon will follow.

The dirge for the dead will be sung for me,
   And the mass be chanted meetly,
And I shall sleep with my little boy,
   In the moonlight churchyard sweetly.

JOHN ANSTER (1793–1867)       

# DOUBLE

Something's happened to my son.
He's not the same child
I breastfed. He was healthy.
I haven't slept in three nights
watching over his cot for signs of a change
when his eyes click open like a china doll.
He can't remember how to be Samuel.
He looks at me as if
I'm not his mother.
His eyes are grey-green.
They say babies' eyes change colour
in the middle of the night.
He used to call me
*Mama*.
Now he only makes noises
I don't understand.

I don't understand.
Now he only makes noises . . .
ma . . . ma.
He used to call me
in the middle of the night.
They say babies' eyes change colour –
his eyes are grey. Green.
I'm not his mother.

He looks at me as if
he can't remember how to be Samuel
when his eyes click open. Like a china doll
watching over his cot for signs of a change,
I haven't slept in three nights.
I breastfed. He was healthy.
He's not the same child.
Something's happened to my son.

# VILLAGE-SONG

Honey, child, honey, child, whither are you going?
Would you cast your jewels all to the breezes
    blowing?
Would you leave the mother who on golden grain
    has fed you?
Would you grieve the lover who is riding forth to
    wed you?

Mother mine, to the wild forest I am going,
Where upon the champa boughs the champa buds are
    blowing;
To the köil-haunted river-isles where lotus lilies
    glisten,
The voices of the fairy folk are calling me –
    O listen!

Honey, child, honey, child, the world is full of pleasure,
Of bridal-songs and cradle-songs and sandal-scented
    leisure.
Your bridal robes are in the loom, silver and saffron
    glowing,
Your bridal cakes are on the hearth: O whither are
    you going?

The bridal-songs and cradle-songs have cadences of
    sorrow,
The laughter of the sun to-day, the wind of death
    to-morrow.
Far sweeter sound the forest-notes where forest-
    streams are falling;
O mother mine, I cannot stay, the fairy-folk are
    calling.

# THE CHANGELING

Toll no bell for me, dear Father, dear Mother,
    Waste no sighs;
There are my sisters, there is my little brother
  Who plays in the place called Paradise,
Your children all, your children for ever;
        But I, so wild,
Your disgrace, with the queer brown face, was never,
  Never, I know, but half your child!

In the garden at play, all day, last summer,
      Far and away I heard
The sweet "tweet-tweet" of a strange new-comer,
  The dearest, clearest call of a bird.
It lived down there in the deep green hollow,
  My own old home, and the fairies say
The word of a bird is a thing to follow,
  So I was away a night and a day.

One evening, too, by the nursery fire,
  We snuggled close and sat round so still,
When suddenly as the wind blew higher,
  Something scratched on the window-sill.
A pinched brown face peered in – I shivered;
  No one listened or seemed to see;
The arms of it waved and the wings of it quivered

Whoo – I knew it had come for me:
  Some are as bad as bad can be!
All night long they danced in the rain,
Round and round in a dripping chain,
Threw their caps at the window-pane,
  Tried to make me scream and shout
  And fling the bedclothes all about:
I meant to stay in bed that night,
And if only you had left a light
  They would never have got me out.

Sometimes I wouldn't speak, you see,
  Or answer when you spoke to me,
Because in the long, still dusks of Spring
You can hear the whole world whispering;
  The shy green grasses making love,
  The feathers grow on the dear, grey dove,
  The tiny heart of the redstart beat,
  The patter of the squirrel's feet,
The pebbles pushing in the silver streams,
The rushes talking in their dreams,
  The swish-swish of the bat's black wings,
  The wild-wood bluebell's sweet ting-tings,
    Humming and hammering at your ear,
    Everything there is to hear
In the heart of hidden things.
  But not in the midst of the nursery riot,

That's why I wanted to be quiet,
 Couldn't do my sums, or sing,
 Or settle down to anything.
 And when, for that, I was sent upstairs
 I *did* kneel down to say my prayers;
But the King who sits on your high church steeple
Has nothing to do with us fairy people!

Times I pleased you, dear Father, dear Mother,
 Learned all my lessons and liked to play,
And dearly loved the little pale brother
 Whom some other bird must have called away.
Why did They bring me here to make me
 Not quite bad and not quite good,
Why, unless They're wicked, do They want, in spite,
  to take me
 Back to their wet, wild wood?
Now, every night I shall see the windows shining,
 The gold lamp's glow, and the fire's red gleam,
While the best of us are twining twigs and the rest of
   us are whining
 In the hollow by the stream.
Black and chill are Their nights on the wold;
 And They live so long and They feel no pain:
I shall grow up, but never grow old,
I shall always, always be very cold,
 I shall never come back again!

# THE CHANGELING

What do you do? He wore his leather jacket to school,
pulled the fire alarm, felt up one of the nuns.
Detention was a time to draw rocket ships
or race cars. He liked things that go fast (skateboards),
things that were secret (cellars), things that squealed
(mice mostly, but also hamsters). He never harmed
    them
but put them in desks, purses, girls' hair.
He read books on poisonous mushrooms and making
    bombs.

What do you do? Tell him, you are a doll,
created from sticks and feathers? Go back where
you came from? He would grin, get your daughter
    pregnant,
set your barn on fire.

# FAIRY SPELLS
AND CHARMS

*Against an elf and against charm-magic:*

*Into wine crumble myrrh and an equal part of frankincense
and shave a part of the stone, jet, into the wine. After
fasting at night, drink this for three or for nine or for
twelve mornings.*

ANONYMOUS Anglo-Saxon Remedy

# THE NIGHT-PIECE, TO JULIA

Her eyes the glow-worm lend thee,
The shooting stars attend thee;
And the elves also,
Whose little eyes glow
Like the sparks of fire, befriend thee.

No Will-o'-th'-Wisp mislight thee,
Nor snake or slow-worm bite thee;
But on, on thy way,
Not making a stay,
Since ghost there's none to affright thee.

Let not the dark thee cumber:
What though the moon does slumber?
The stars of the night
Will lend thee their light
Like tapers clear without number.

Then, Julia, let me woo thee,
Thus, thus to come unto me;
And when I shall meet
Thy silv'ry feet
My soul I'll pour into thee.

ROBERT HERRICK (1591 – 1674)

## GAELIC CHARM AGAINST
## FAIRY INFLUENCE

We accept their protection,
We repudiate their (evil) tricks,
(May) their back (be) to us, their face from us
Through merit of the passion and death of our Saviour.

ANONYMOUS
TRANSLATED BY WILLIAM MACKENZIE


## SONG TO QUELL THE ELF

I have wreathed round the wounds
The best of healing wreaths
That the baneful sores may
Neither burn nor burst,
Nor find their way further,
Nor turn foul and fallow,
Nor thump and throle on,
Nor be wicked wounds,
Nor dig deeply down:
But he himself may hold
In a way to health.
Let it ache thee no more
Than ear in Earth acheth.

178 ANONYMOUS *The Leech Book of Bald*
(*c.* 9TH CENTURY) TRANSLATED BY
FELIX GRENDON

# AYRE XVIII

Thrice tosse these Oaken ashes in the ayre,
Thrice sit thou mute in this inchanted chayre;
And thrice three times tye vp this true loues knot,
And murmur soft, shee will, or shee will not.

Goe burn these poys'nous weedes in yon blew fire,
These Screech-owles fethers and this prickling bryer;
This Cypresse gathered at a dead mans graue;
That all thy feares and cares, an end may haue.

Then come, you Fayries, dance with me a round;
Melt her hard hart with your melodious sound:
In vaine are all the charms I can deuise:
She hath an Arte to breake them with her eyes.

# THE ROMANCE OF THE FAIRY CURE

Nelly Phelan's child is ailing;
Hour by hour, the babe is failing;
Squeeling, kicking, biting, whining,
To an atomy he's pining.

Once he was a fine, wee fellow;
Now he's wrinkled, thin, and yellow.
Playful then he was, and civil;
Now he's cross-grained, as the devil.

To a wise woman Nell's walking;
Long time they're in secret talking;
First she heard all Nell's description;
Then she wrote out a prescription.

"Take this cure, although a strange one;
It is needed when they change one;
By it you'll the fairies bother,
Get your child, and choke the other.

"You must make the fairy speak out,
Ere your child, from them, you take out.
If you follow what's here written,
You shall find the biter bitten."

Cried Nell, "Be sure that I'll observe it;
If I fail I'll not deserve it:
I would walk the wide world over,
If my child I could recover."

Five hundred egg-shells Nelly chooses
In a pot, the shells she bruises;
In spring water now they're boiling,
Stirring round the pot she's toiling.

Red-hot now the poker's ready;
While Nell stirs the pot, so steady:
From the child, in cradle lying,
Nell now hears a strange voice crying –

"Mammy! Mammy! what's that boiling?
Why with potstick are you toiling?"
Nell, with fright, to drop was ready,
Yet she answered, cool, and steady –

"Egg-shells, deary! I am brewing,
Cock's broth for my babe I'm stewing.
When I skim off all the dripping,
Then it will be fit for sipping."

"Though five hundred years I'm chewing,
Egg-shells never saw I brewing;
Though five centuries I'm cheating,
Ne'er have I seen cock's broth eating."

Quick the poker Nelly seizes;
To the cradle now she races;
Red-hot down its throat she crams it;
With her might and main she rams it.

Gone like lightning is the fairy;
In its stead, there lies her deary –
Her brave boy – her darling Terry,
With his lip and cheek of cherry.

From THE ORDINARY

Saint Francis and Saint Benedict,
Bless this house from wicked wight;
From the Night-mare and the Goblin
That is hight Good-Fellow Robin;
Keep it from all evil spirits,
Fairies, weasels, rats, and ferrets,
From curfew-time
To the next prime.

# From NYMPHIDIA: THE FAIRY COURT

"By the croaking of the frog;
By the howling of the dog;
By the crying of the hog
    Against the storm arising;
By the evening curfew-bell;
By the doleful dying knell;
O let this my direful spell,
    Hob, hinder thy surprising.

"By the Mandrake's dreadful groans;
By the Lubrican's sad moans;
By the noise of dead men's bones
    In charnel houses rattling;
By the hissing of the snake,
The rustling of the fire-drake,
I charge thee this place forsake,
    Nor of Queen Mab be prattling.

"By the whirlwind's hollow sound,
By the thunder's dreadful stound,
Yells of spirits underground,
    I charge thee not to fear us:
By the screech-owl's dismal note,
By the black night-raven's throat,
I charge thee, Hob, to tear thy coat
    With thorns, if thou come near us."

184   MICHAEL DRAYTON (1563–1631)

# THE FAIRY BEAM UPON YOU

The fairy beam upon you,
The stars to glister on you,
  A moon of light
  In the noon of night,
Till the firedrake hath o'er-gone you.
The wheel of fortune guide you,
The boy with the bow beside you
Run aye in the way
  Till the bird of day
And the luckier lote betide you.

BEN JONSON (1572–1637)                    185

# ABSINTHE, THE
# GREEN FAIRY

*Absinthe has a wonderful colour, green. A glass of absinthe
is as poetical as anything in the world.*

OSCAR WILDE (1854–1900)

*It is difficult to me sometimes to keep my thoughts in
sequence. No absintheur can be always coherent; it is too
much to expect of the green fairy's votaries!*

MARIE CORELLI, *Wormwood: A Drama of Paris* (1890)

*His breath hangs over our saucestained plates, the green
fairy's fang thrusting between his lips . . . Green eyes, I see
you. Fang, I feel.*

JAMES JOYCE, *Ulysses* (1922)

# THE POISON

Wine knows how to decorate the Evil Houses
With a luxury miraculous,
And to make surge from a sunset fabulous
The red gold, where the hot sun drowses
Before he falls into the Ocean perilous.

Opium heightens our unlimited Illusions
Beyond Eternity,
Deepens Time, hollows Sensuality,
And, with the pleasures of our Delusions,
Fills the soul beyond its own captivity.

All that is not worth the poison that is distilling
From thy green eyes, to clash on
Clouds when my soul trembles in an inverse passion;
My dreams as visions stilling
Their thirst in the bitter gulfs of furious fashion.

Nothing is worth the horrible projection
Of thy saliva, thy breath is
About to plunge my soul where Hades' wraith is,
And, *charioting* the creation,
Hurls it hideously where its ultimate Death is!

CHARLES BAUDELAIRE (1821–67)                    189
TRANSLATED BY ARTHUR SYMONS

## ANOTHER LINEAGE

Eros, I want to guide you, blind Father . . .
From your almighty hands I ask for
His sublime body spilled in fire
Upon my body faint in roses!

The electric corolla that I now open
Offers the nectary of a garden of wives;
To his vultures in my flesh I offer
A whole swarm of roseate doves.

Give to the two cruel serpents of his embrace
My great feverish stem . . . Absinth, honeys,
Spill on me from his veins, from his mouth . . .

This lying I am an ardent furrow
Where can be nurtured the seed
Of another lineage sublimely mad!

DELMIRA AGUSTINI (1886–1914)
TRANSLATED BY ALEJANDRO CÁCERES

# RHENISH NIGHT

My glass is full of shivering wine aflame
Listen to the bargeman's moonlight lento
Seven maidens all in a row
Twist their long green manes

Get up Sing louder Dance around
Eclipse the moonlight lento
Smother me with many blondes
Braided hair and eyes without emotion

The Rhine is drunk where the vineyards gleam
The coinage of the night is drowned
Death rattles in the singing stream
Green-haired witches sing the summer round

My wineglass splits its sides with laughter

GUILLAUME APOLLINAIRE (1880–1918)          191
TRANSLATED BY DONALD REVELL

## THE VAIN DANCERS

They who are as light as flowers came,
Golden figurines and beauties in miniature
Irised by a pallid moon. . . . See how they
Glide away like tunes into the clear wood.
Of mallow, and iris, and nocturnal roses
Are the night charms that blossom beneath their
    dances.
How many veiled perfumes are shed by their gold
    fingers!
But the soft azure disleafs in this dead grove
And a thin water scarcely gleams, laid there
Like a pale treasury of ancient dew
Whence silence rises like a flower. . . . See them anew
Glide away like tunes into the clear wood.
To the loved flower-cups their hands are gracious;
A ghost of moon slumbers on their devout lips
And their marvelous arms with gestures sleep-lulled
Love to unwind under the friendly myrtles
Their wild enlacings and their caresses. . . . But one
    or two,
Less captive to the rhythm and the remote harps,
Make off on subtle step towards the buried lake
To drink the lilies' frail draught where pure oblivion
    sleeps.

PAUL VALÉRY (1871 – 1945)
    TRANSLATED BY DAVID PAUL

## ABSINTHE

Absinthe! It came and the glass was filled
for the third time I believe, if memory serves,
for, I thought, here is cure to be found
and I was ill in body and in mind.

The green witch's caress was so soft,
that heart tired of life forgot its troubles.
Absinthe is good: you feel it in marrow and bone
and it livens more than all the doctor's pills.

And now a nymph! In the mud of the boulevard
I find myself a friend for the night.
By her embrace the image of Dagny shall flee
like the morning mist flees from the water of the
      Seine.

A kiss and yet one more! Champagne too –
let the wine flow! – Hello, we shall drink,
until all memories vanish in drunkenness
and we be blessed like gods, girl!

That's how I live, and fall more and more,
and the rift widens during the night hours,
until I for sheer dark cannot see
how friendly the far northern star glimmers.

Yet often the morning sun finds me
in dumb despair leaned at my desk.
Then I love over again and worship you,
and the story begins, where I thought it ended.

194   CARL DANIEL FÄLLSTRÖM (1858–1937)
TRANSLATED BY MARKUS HARTSMAR

# L'ABSINTHE

Absinthe, I adore you truly!
It seems when I drink you,
I inhale the young forest's soul,
During the beautiful green season.

Your perfume disconcerts me
And in your opalescence
I see the full heavens of yore,
As through an open door.

What matter, O refuge of the damned!
That you a vain paradise be,
If you appease my need;

And if, before I enter the door,
You make me put up with life,
By accustoming me to death.

RAOUL PONCHON (1848—1937)
TRANSLATED BY MARKUS HARTSMAR

# I AM THE GREEN FAIRY

I am the Green Fairy
My robe is the color of despair
I have nothing in common with the fairies of the
past
What I need is blood, red and hot, the palpitating
flesh of my victims
Alone, I will kill France, the Present is dead, Vive
the Future . . .
But me, I kill the future and in the family I destroy
the love of country, courage, honor,
I am the purveyor of hell, penitentiaries, hospitals.
Who am I finally? I am the instigator of crime
I am ruin and sorrow
I am shame
I am dishonor
I am death
I am absinthe

ANONYMOUS (Anti-Alcohol League, *c.* 1900)

# SYMBOLIC FAIRIES

*Who knows, but that in every brain may dwell*
*Those creatures we call fairies? Who can tell?*
*And by their several actions they may frame*
*Those forms and figures, which we fancies call.*

MARGARET CAVENDISH, "Of Fairies in the
Brain" (1668)

# FROM THE SOMME

In other days I sang of simple things,
 Of summer dawn, and summer noon and night,
The dewy grass, the dew-wet fairy rings,
  The lark's long golden flight.

Deep in the forest I made melody
 While squirrels cracked their hazel nuts on high,
Or I would cross the wet sand to the sea
  And sing to sea and sky.

When came the silvered silence of the night
 I stole to casements over scented lawns,
And softly sang of love and love's delight
  To mute white marble fauns.

Oft in the tavern parlour I would sing
 Of morning sun upon the mountain vine,
And, calling for a chorus, sweep the string
  In praise of good red wine.

I played with all the toys the gods provide,
 I sang my songs and made glad holiday.
Now I have cast my broken toys aside
  And flung my lute away.

A singer once, I now am fain to weep.
  Within my soul I feel strange music swell,
Vast chants of tragedy too deep – too deep
      For my poor lips to tell.

# SPOILS OF THE DEAD

Two fairies it was
  On a still summer day
Came forth in the woods
  With the flowers to play.

The flowers they plucked
  They cast on the ground
For others, and those
  For still others they found.

Flower-guided it was
  That they came as they ran
On something that lay
  In the shape of a man.

The snow must have made
  The feathery bed
When this one fell
  On the sleep of the dead.

But the snow was gone
  A long time ago,
And the body he wore
  Nigh gone with the snow.

The fairies drew near
    And keenly espied
A ring on his hand
    And a chain at his side.

They knelt in the leaves
    And eerily played
With the glittering things,
    And were not afraid.

And when they went home
    To hide in their burrow,
They took them along
    To play with to-morrow.

When *you* came on death,
    Did you not come flower-guided
Like the elves in the wood?
    I remember that I did.

But I recognised death
    With sorrow and dread,
And I hated and hate
    The spoils of the dead.

## SILENCE
(*To Eleonora Duse*)

We are anhungered after solitude,
Deep stillness pure of any speech or sound,
Soft quiet hovering over pools profound,
The silences that on the desert brood,
Above a windless hush of empty seas,
The broad unfurling banners of the dawn;
A faëry forest where there sleeps a Faun;
Our souls are fain of solitudes like these.
O woman who divined our weariness,
And set the crown of silence on your art,
From what undreamed-of depth within your heart
Have you sent forth the hush that makes us free
To hear an instant, high above earth's stress,
The silent music of infinity?

SARA TEASDALE (1884 – 1933)

# HOLIDAYS

The holiest of all holidays are those
   Kept by ourselves in silence and apart;
   The secret anniversaries of the heart,
   When the full river of feeling overflows; –
The happy days unclouded to their close;
   The sudden joys that out of darkness start
   As flames from ashes; swift desires that dart
   Like swallows singing down each wind that blows!
White as the gleam of a receding sail,
   White as a cloud that floats and fades in air,
   White as the whitest lily on a stream,
These tender memories are; – a fairy tale
   Of some enchanted land we know not where,
   But lovely as a landscape in a dream.

# DREAMS WITHIN DREAMS

I have gone out and seen the lands of Faery
    And have found sorrow and peace and beauty there,
And have not known one from the other, but found
      each
    Lovely and gracious alike, delicate and fair.

"They are children of one mother, she that is called
      Longing,
    Desire, Love," one told me: and another, "her secret
    name
Is Wisdom:" and another, "they are not three but one:"
    And another, "touch them not, seek them not, they
      are wind and flame."

I have come back from the hidden, silent lands of
      Faery
    And have forgotten the music of its ancient streams:
And now flame and wind and the long, grey,
      wandering wave
    And beauty and peace and sorrow are dreams
      within dreams.

FIONA MACLEOD (WILLIAM SHARPE)       205
(1855 – 1905)

# IN THE PICTURE GALLERY

With palette laden
   She sat, as I passed her,
A dainty maiden
   Before an Old Master.

What mountain-top is
   She bent upon? Ah,
She neatly copies
   Murillo's Madonna.

But rapt and brimming
   The eyes' full chalice says
The heart builds dreaming
   Its fairy-palaces.

\*   \*   \*

The eighteenth year rolled
   By, ere returning,
I greeted the dear old
   Scenes with yearning.

With palette laden
   She sat, as I passed her,
A faded maiden
   Before an Old Master.

But what is she doing?
    The same thing still – lo,
Hotly pursuing
    That very Murillo!

Her wrist never falters;
    It keeps her, that poor wrist,
With panels for altars
    And daubs for the tourist.

And so she has painted
    Through years unbrightened,
Till hopes have fainted
    And hair has whitened.

But rapt and brimming
    The eyes' full chalice says
The heart builds dreaming
    Its fairy-palaces.

HENRIK JOHAN IBSEN (1828–1906)                207
TRANSLATED BY FYDELL EDMUND GARRETT

# TO MY FAIRY FANCIES

Nay, no longer I may hold you,
    In my spirit's soft caresses,
Nor like lotus-leaves enfold you
    In the tangles of my tresses.
Fairy fancies, fly away
    To the white cloud-wildernesses,
            Fly away!

Nay, no longer ye may linger
    With your laughter-lighted faces,
Now I am a thought-worn singer
    In life's high and lonely places.
Fairy fancies, fly away,
    To bright wind-inwoven spaces,
            Fly away!

# UNWRITTEN POEMS

Fairy spirits of the breeze –
Frailer nothing is than these.
Fancies born we know not where –
In the heart or in the air;
Wandering echoes blown unsought
From far crystal peaks of thought;
Shadows, fading at the dawn,
Ghosts of feeling dead and gone:
Alas! Are all fair things that live
Still lovely and still fugitive?

WILLIAM WINTER (1836–1917)                    209

# THE SICK MUSE

Poor Muse, alas, what ails thee, then, to-day?
Thy hollow eyes with midnight visions burn,
Upon thy brow in alternation play,
Folly and Horror, cold and taciturn.

Have the green lemure and the goblin red,
Poured on thee love and terror from their urn?
Or with despotic hand the nightmare dread
Deep plunged thee in some fabulous Minturne?

Would that thy breast where so deep thoughts arise,
Breathed forth a healthful perfume with thy sighs;
Would that thy Christian blood ran wave by wave

In rhythmic sounds the antique numbers gave,
When Phœbus shared his alternating reign
With mighty Pan, lord of the ripening grain.

## ANOTHER

'Tis a moon-tinted primrose, with a well
   Of trembling dew; in its soft atmosphere,
A tiny whirlwind of sweet smells, doth dwell
   A ladybird; and when no sound is near
That elfin hermit fans the fairy bell
   With glazen wings, (mirrors on which appear
Atoms of colours that flizz by unseen,)
   And struts about his darling flower with pride.
But, if some buzzing gnat with pettish spleen
   Come whining by, the insect 'gins to hide,
And folds its flimsy drapery between
   His speckled buckler and soft, silken side.
     So poets fly the critic's snappish heat,
     And sheath their minds in scorn and self-conceit.

From POST IMPRESSIONS

## VI

at the head of this street a gasping organ is waving
moth-eaten tunes.  a fattish hand turns the crank;
the box sprouts fairies, out of it sour gnomes tumble
clumsily, the little box is spilling rancid elves upon
neat sunlight into the flower-stricken air which is filthy
with agile swarming sonal creatures

– Children, stand with circular frightened faces glar-
ing at the shabby tiny smiling, man in whose hand the
crank goes desperately, round and round pointing to
the queer monkey

(if you toss him a coin he will pick it cleverly from,
the air and stuff it seriously in, his minute pocket)
Sometimes he does not catch a piece of money and then
his master will yell at him over the music and jerk the
little string and the monkey will sit, up, and look at,
you with his solemn blinky eyeswhichneversmile and
after he has caught a, penny or three, pennies he will be
thrown a peanut (which he will open skilfully with his,
mouth carefully holding, it, in his little toylike hand)
and then he will stiff-ly throw the shell away with a
small bored gesture that makes the children laugh.

But i don't,    the crank goes round desperate elves and
hopeless gnomes and frantic fairies gush clumsily from
the battered box fattish and mysterious the flower-
stricken sunlight is thickening dizzily is reeling gently
the street and the children and the monkeyandthe-
organ and the man are dancing slowly are tottering up
and down in a trembly mist of atrocious melody . . . .
tiniest dead tunes crawl upon my face my hair is lousy
with mutilated singing microscopic things in my ears
scramble faintly tickling putrescent atomies,
            and
                i feel the jerk of the little string! the
tiny smiling shabby man is yelling over the music
i understand him i shove my round red hat back on
my head i sit up and blink at you with my solemn
eyeswhichneversmile

yes, By god.
for i am they are pointing at the queer monkey with a
little oldish doll-like face and hairy arms like an ogre
and rubbercoloured hands and feet filled with quick
fingers and a remarkable tail which is allbyitself alive.
(and he has a little red coat with i have a real pocket
in it and the round funny hat with a big feather is tied
under myhis chin.) that climbs and cries and runs and
floats like a toy on the end of a string

# THE FAIRY

"Come hither, my Sparrows,
My little arrows.
If a tear or a smile
Will a man beguile,
If an amorous delay
Clouds a sunshiny day,
If the step of a foot
Smites the heart to its root,
'Tis the marriage ring –
Makes each fairy a king."

So a Fairy sung.
From the leaves I sprung;
He leap'd from the spray
To flee away;
But in my hat caught,
He soon shall be taught.
Let him laugh, let him cry,
He's my Butterfly;
For I've pull'd out the sting
Of the marriage-ring.

## LIED DER LIEBE (SONG OF LOVE)

Past spruces on hillsides, through alders by the brook
your image, beloved, follows me always.
To me it smiles now love, now peace
in the kindly glimmer of the moon.

In the brightness of early morning your fair form
      arises
from the rose bushes in the garden;
it floats from the crimson-flowering mountains
like an Elysian shadow.

Often in dreams I have seen you,
the loveliest of fairies, radiant on your golden throne;
often I have glimpsed you, spirited to lofty Olympus,
as Hebe among the gods.

From the depths, from the heights I hear
your heavenly name echo like music of the spheres;
I imagine the scent enveloping the blossom
shot through with your melodious voice.

At midnight's holy hour my prescient mind
floats through the realms of the ether.
Beloved! There a land beckons
where lover and beloved are forever reunited.

Joy vanishes, no sorrow endures;
the years flow away in the river of time;
the sun will die, the earth perish:
but love must last for ever and ever.

216   FRIEDRICH VON MATTHISSON (1761–1831)
TRANSLATED BY RICHARD WIGMORE

# QUICKTHORN

Don't bring haw into the house at night
or in any month with a red fruit in season
or when starlings bank against the light,
don't bring haw in. Don't give me reason
to think you have hidden haw about you.
Tucked in secret, may its thorn thwart you.
Plucked in blossom, powdered by your thumb,
I will smell it for the hum of haw is long,
its hold is low and lilting. If you bring
haw in, I will know you want me gone
to the fairies and their jilting. I will know
you want me buried in the deep green field
where god knows what is rotting.

SIOBHAN CAMPBELL (1962– )

## SORROWING LOVE

And again the flowers are come
And the light shakes,
And no tiny voice is dumb,
And a bud breaks
On the humble bush and the proud restless tree.
Come with me!

Look, this little flower is pink,
And this one white.
Here's a pearl cup for your drink,
Here's for your delight
A yellow one, sweet with honey,
Here's fairy money
Silver bright
Scattered over the grass
As we pass.

Here's moss. How the smell of it lingers
On my cold fingers!
You shall have no moss. Here's a frail
Hyacinth, deathly pale.
Not for you, not for you!
And the place where they grew
You must promise me not to discover,
My sorrowful lover!

Shall we never be happy again?
Never again play?
In vain – in vain!
Come away!

# OLD DWARF HEART

True. All too true. I have never been at home in life.
All my decay has taken place upon a child.
*Henderson the Rain King*, by SAUL BELLOW


When I lie down to love,
old dwarf heart shakes her head.
Like an imbecile she was born old,
Her eyes wobble as thirty-one thick folds
of skin open to glare at me on my flickering bed.
She knows the decay we're made of.

When hurt she is abrupt.
Now she is solid, like fat,
breathing in loops like a green hen
in the dust. But if I dream of loving, then
my dreams are of snarling strangers. *She* dreams
        that . . .
strange, strange, and corrupt.

Good God, the things she knows!
And worse, the sores she holds
in her hands, gathered in like a nest
from an abandoned field. At her best
she is all red muscle, humming in and out, cajoled
by time. Where I go, she goes.

Oh now I lay me down to love,
how awkwardly her arms undo,
how patiently I untangle her wrists
like knots. Old ornament, old naked fist,
even if I put on seventy coats I could not cover you . . .
mother, father, I'm made of.

# MYTHS OF THE DISAPPEARANCE

I rise like a red balloon, untethered and vacant.

The essence of my dolor has become rarefied,
Holy; like a fragrance, bodiless, without referent.
It is a pale shadow on the sun, a wasp's-wing,
    accidental
Splash of poison on the white rose's thorn –
I twist it in my fingers and faint. *Shall I tell you?*

There was one bad fairy at my birth, there came one
    curse,
One blister, one drop of mercury in the moult of me
And everything was ruined after.

                            Still it is
No good; the words drift from me like ashes.
I am so old now, I have left half my life
In caves hollowed out in rock by the seashore:
I prayed in each one, and could not find my way back,
Or lied when the pass-word was asked, or turned my
    back,
Making gestures of despondency at the roiling surf.

                    In a mirror I shot all my hateful selves,
                                    the yesterdays.

# LINES TO MY FATHER

The many sow, but only the chosen reap;
Happy the wretched host if Day be brief,
That with the cool oblivion of sleep
A dawnless Night may soothe the smart of grief.

If from the soil our sweat enriches sprout
One meagre blossom for our hands to cull,
Accustomed indigence provokes a shout
Of praise that life becomes so bountiful.

Now ushered regally into your own,
Look where you will, as far as eye can see,
Your little seeds are to a fullness grown,
And golden fruit is ripe on every tree.

Yours is no fairy gift, no heritage
Without travail, to which weak wills aspire;
This is a merited and grief-earned wage
From One Who holds His servants worth their hire.

So has the shyest of your dreams come true,
Built not of sand, but of the solid rock,
Impregnable to all that may accrue
Of elemental rage: storm, stress, and shock.

COUNTEE CULLEN (1903–46)                    223

# ESCAPE

When foxes eat the last gold grape,
And the last white antelope is killed,
I shall stop fighting and escape
Into a little house I'll build.

But first I'll shrink to fairy size,
With a whisper no one understands,
Making blind moons of all your eyes,
And muddy roads of all your hands.

And you may grope for me in vain
In hollows under the mangrove root,
Or where, in apple-scented rain,
The silver wasp-nests hang like fruit.

## From VISIONS

A rose, as fair as ever saw the North,
Grew in a little garden all alone;
A sweeter flower did Nature ne'er put forth,
Nor fairer garden yet was never known:
The maidens danc'd about it morn and noon,
And learned bards of it their ditties made;
The nimble fairies by the pale-fac'd moon
Water'd the root and kiss'd her pretty shade.
But well-a-day, the gard'ner careless grew;
The maids and fairies both were kept away,
And in a drought the caterpillars threw
Themselves upon the bud and every spray.
   God shield the stock! if heaven send no supplies,
    The fairest blossom of the garden dies.

WILLIAM BROWNE (*c.* 1590–*c.* 1645)

# A LITTLE BUDDING ROSE

It was a little budding rose,
Round like a fairy globe,
And shyly did its leaves unclose
Hid in their mossy robe,
But sweet was the slight and spicy smell
It breathed from its heart invisible.

The rose is blasted, withered, blighted,
Its root has felt a worm,
And like a heart beloved and slighted,
Failed, faded, shrunk its form.
Bud of beauty, bonnie flower,
I stole thee from thy natal bower.

I was the worm that withered thee,
Thy tears of dew all fell for me;
Leaf and stalk and rose are gone,
Exile earth they died upon.
Yes, that last breath of balmy scent
With alien breezes sadly blent!

226   EMILY BRONTË (1818—48)

# SONNET LXIII: THE GOSSAMER

O'er faded heath-flowers spun, or thorny furze,
   The filmy Gossamer is lightly spread;
Waving in every sighing air that stirs,
   As Fairy fingers had entwined the thread:
A thousand trembling orbs of lucid dew
   Spangle the texture of the fairy loom,
As if soft Sylphs, lamenting as they flew,
   Had wept departed Summer's transient bloom:
But the wind rises, and the turf receives
   The glittering web: – So, evanescent, fade
Bright views that Youth with sanguine heart, believes:
   So vanish schemes of bliss, by Fancy made;
Which, fragile as the fleeting dreams of morn,
Leave but the wither'd heath, and barren thorn!

CHARLOTTE SMITH (1749–1806)

# WITHIN MY GARDEN, RIDES A BIRD

Within my Garden, rides a Bird
Upon a single Wheel –
Whose spokes a dizzy Music make
As 'twere a travelling Mill –

He never stops, but slackens
Above the Ripest Rose –
Partakes without alighting
And praises as he goes,

Till every spice is tasted –
And then his Fairy Gig
Reels in remoter atmospheres –
And I rejoin my Dog,

And He and I, perplex us
If positive, 'twere we –
Or bore the Garden in the Brain
This Curiosity –

But He, the best Logician,
Refers my clumsy eye –
To just vibrating Blossoms!
An Exquisite Reply!

228   EMILY DICKINSON (1830–66)

# ACROSS THE BORDER

*I have read somewhere that the birds of fairyland are white as snow.* — W. B. YEATS

Where all the trees bear golden flowers,
  And all the birds are white;
Where fairy folk in dancing hours
  Burn stars for candlelight;

Where every wind and leaf can talk,
  But no man understand
Save one whose child-feet chanced to walk
  Green paths of fairyland;

I followed two swift silver wings;
  I stalked a roving song;
I startled shining, silent things;
  I wandered all day long.

But when it seemed the shadowy hours
  Whispered of soft-foot night,
I crept home to sweet common flowers,
  Brown birds, and candlelight.

SOPHIE JEWETT (1861–1909)                    229

# FATE OF THE
# FAIRIES

*Methinks there are no goblins, and men's talk*
*That in these Woods the Nimble Fairies walk*
*Are fables.*

JOHN FLETCHER, *The Faithful Shepherdess* (*c.* 1609)

*In the old days of King Arthur,*
*Whom the Britons speak of with such great honour,*
*All this land was filled with fayries.*
*The elf-queen, with her jolly company,*
*Danced often in many a green mede,*
*This was the old opinion, as I have read.*
*I speak of many hundred years ago;*
*But now no man can see elves anymore.*

GEOFFREY CHAUCER, From *The Canterbury Tales* (1392)

*What joy were diminished on the earth*
*If Faeries ceased from being?*

JANE BARLOW, From *The End of Elfintown* (1894)

# FAIRY DISTANCE

There behind the tree beautiful saw-teeth were
    singing unseen
In the space between clouds there were shapely ears
Iridescent painted nails dissolved in water
The tiny discarded stones
Like footprints everything even
The wind was getting lost
In a leaned-back over-turned chair
The crazed ingress to a wheat field
The labyrinth made of air
There is not a single card
There is not a single glass
Like in a stringed instrument of desire
The strange line pierced it
It just barely looked like the innocent expression
    of a little finch
It will live like a death buoy
In the spring wind
It just barely looked like the equilibrium of the
    English sparrow

SHŪZŌ TAKIGUCHI (1903–79)    233
TRANSLATED BY MARY JO BANG AND
YUKI TANAKA

# THE LOST FAIRIES

They come no more with the dancing feet,
Where the daffodil chorus rang sweet, so sweet;
Fairies o' mine, have ye fled for ever?
Shall we meet no more as we used to meet?

The come no more and the wheels run slow,
And the laughter is hushed that I used to know;
The white owl cries in the twilit meadow
Where our revels rang in the long ago.

O a fairy came knocking one day, one day,
At the meadowsweet gate where we used to play –
I heard him knock, but my heart was weary,
And I sent him weeping away, away.

And ever since then, tho' my heart be sore
With waiting and watching, they come no more;
And the lilies have stolen their golden sandals,
And the poppies are flaunting the gowns they wore.

Ah! ever since then, in the noon o' the flowers,
When the lights are soft in the fairy bowers,
I sigh and sigh for the banished laughter,
For the singing soul of the wasted hours.

Do they mourn me, I wonder, as one that passed
While the sentinel snapdragons slumbered fast?
Or is it they seek me, all loyal-hearted,
And dream they shall find me at last, at last?

I know not; ever the red suns rise
And roll to their rest in the western skies,
But the loved, lost voices are silent, silent,
And leaps no light to the darkened eyes.

Only when twilight lifteth her wand
And turneth the glory to shadowland,
I hear in the stillness a sound of weeping –
And know the meaning, and understand.

They have passed the boundaries mortals know,
Where the asphodel blooms and the dream-stars
        glow,
Tho' I seek them, seek them till suns be ashes,
I shall never find them wherever I go.

They will come no more with the dancing feet,
Where the daffodil chorus rang sweet, so sweet;
Where the white owl cries in the haunted meadow,
We shall meet no more as we used to meet.

# GOLDEN FAIRIES

Golden fairies
In a satin garden!
When will I find
The icy avenues?
Silvery splashes of
Infatuated naiads,
Where are the jealous boards
That will block your way.
Lit by fire,
The dusk has frozen
Over the flight of fancies.
Beyond the gloom of curtains
There are funeral urns,
And an azure vault of
Deceitful stars doesn't wait.

TRANSLATED BY RONALD E. PETERSON

## XXI

The fairies break their dances
　　And leave the printed lawn,
And up from India glances
　　The silver sail of dawn.

The candles burn their sockets,
　　The blinds let through the day,
The young man feels his pockets
　　And wonders what's to pay.

A. E. HOUSMAN (1859−1936)

## AFTER MANY SPRINGS

Now,
In June,
When the night is a vast softness
Filled with blue stars,
And broken shafts of moon-glimmer
Fall upon the earth,
Am I too old to see the fairies dance?
I cannot find them any more.

# FAREWELL REWARDS AND FAIRIES

Farewell rewards and fairies,
  Good housewives now may say,
For now foul sluts in dairies
  Do fare as well as they.
And though they sweep their hearths no less
  Than maids were wont to do,
Yet who of late for cleanliness,
  Finds sixpence in her shoe?

Lament, lament, old abbeys,
  The fairies lost command;
They did but change priests' babies,
  But some have changed your land;
And all your children sprung from thence
  Are now grown Puritans;
Who live as changelings ever since,
  For love of your domains.

At morning and at evening both,
  You merry were and glad,
So little care of sleep or sloth
  These pretty ladies had;
When Tom came home from labour,
  Or Cis to milking rose,
Then merrily went their tabour,
  And nimbly went their toes.

Witness those rings and roundelays
    Of theirs, which yet remain,
Were footed in Queen Mary's days
    On many a grassy plain;
But since of late, Elizabeth,
    And later, James came in,
They never danced on any heath
    As when the time hath been.

By which we note the fairies
    Were of the old profession,
Their songs were Ave Maries,
    Their dances were procession:
But now, alas! they all are dead,
    Or gone beyond the seas;
Or farther for religion fled,
    Or else they take their ease.

A tell-tale in their company
    They never could endure,
And whoso kept not secretly
    Their mirth, was punished sore;
It was a just and Christian deed
    To pinch such black and blue:
Oh, how the Commonwealth doth need
    Such justices as you.

# From THE EMIGRATION OF THE SPRITES

## I

There was a time, in Anglo land,
When goblin grim, and fairy fair,
On earth, in water, and in air,
Held undisturbed command.
Ye hills and groves! lament, in grief –
Lament, and say, woe worth the day,
When innovating disbelief
First drove the friendly sprites away;
Then was there not a forest leaf
Without attendant elfin grey,
That sat to make the leaflet shake,
Whene'er the breezes chose to wake.

## II

There was not, then, a forest lawn
Where fairy ringlet was not made,
Before, through the surrounding shade,
The slanting sun bespoke the dawn.
There was no knoll beneath an oak
Where were not found, bestrewed around,
By woodman's child (from slumber woke
By singing birds' delightful sound)
Pink tops, from mushroom tables broke,
And acorn cups upon the ground,

From which so fine, when fairies dine,
They always drink their dewy wine.

### III
There was no fell or misty mountain,
Beneath whose darkling cliffs, at night,
There brooded not some shadowy sprite:
There was no swiftly flowing fountain
Without a spirit to preside;
And, on the moor and by the fen,
The kelpie by the water-side,
(The bane of all wayfaring men)
Shook his bright torch, a faithless guide;
The brownie wandered in the glen,
Or stalked upon the hill-top high,
Gigantic on the evening sky. . . .

### XIII
Deserted England! now no more
Inspiring spirits haunt thy hills;
Nor spiritual being fills
Thy mountain æther as of yore.
No more shall fancy find its food
In torrent's song, or tempest's roar;
Or hear a voice in solitude,
On hill and dale, by sea or shore.

No more shall Scotland's peasant rude
Recount his legendary lore;
The soul of Poesie is fled,
And fancy's sacred fire is dead.

JOHN RUSKIN (1819 – 1900)

# FAIRIES' RECALL

While the blue is richest
  In the starry sky,
While the softest shadows
  On the greensward lie,
While the moonlight slumbers
  In the lily's urn,
Bright elves of the wild wood!
  Oh! return, return!

Round the forest fountain,
  On the river shore,
Let your silvery laughter
  Echo yet once more;
While the joyous bounding
  Of your dewy feet
Rings to that old chorus:
  "The daisy is so sweet!"

Oberon, Titania,
  Did your starlight mirth,
With the song of Avon,
  Quit this work-day earth?
Yet while green leaves glisten,
  And while bright stars burn,
By that magic memory,
  Oh, return, return!

# DOUBT NO MORE THAT OBERON

Doubt no more that Oberon —
Never doubt that Pan
Lived, and played a reed, and ran
After nymphs in a dark forest,
In the merry, credulous days, —
Lived, and led a fairy band
Over the indulgent land!

Ah, for in this dourest, sorest
Age man's eye has looked upon,
Death to fauns and death to fays,
Still the dog-wood dares to raise —
Healthy tree, with trunk and root —
Ivory bowls that bear no fruit,
And the starlings and the jays —
Birds that cannot even sing —
Dare to come again in spring!

EDNA ST. VINCENT MILLAY (1892 – 1950)                245

# BELIEF

We do not know
If there be fairies now
   Or no.
But why should we ourselves involve
In questions which we cannot solve.
   O let's pretend it's so
And then perhaps if we are good
Some day we'll see them in the wood.

# ACKNOWLEDGMENTS

Thanks are due to the following copyright holders for permission to reprint:

PATIENCE AGBABI: "Double". Simon Trewin Limited. DELMIRA AGUSTINI: "Another Lineage". In *Selected Poetry of Delmira Agustini: Poetics of Eros.* Edited and translated by Alejandro Cáceres. Carbondale: Southern Illinois University Press, 2003. Copyright © 2003 by the Board of Trustees, Southern Illinois University. Reprinted with permission. ANONYMOUS: "Lovely Lady". In Gabriel Rosenstock, *Treasury of Irish Love Poems, Proverbs and Triads.* New York: Hippocrene Books, 1998. Copyright © 1998 by Hippocrene Books, Inc. Translation copyright © by Gabriel Rosenstock. GUILLAUME APOLLINAIRE: "Rhenish Night" from *Alcools* by Guillaume Apollinaire, translated by Donald Revell. Copyright © 1995 by Donald Revell. Reprinted by permission of Wesleyan University Press. W. H. AUDEN: "Belief". In Ed. Katherine Bucknell, *W. H. Auden Juvenilia: Poems 1922–1928.* Princeton: Princeton University Press, 1994. Copyright © 1994 by The Estate of W. H. Auden. Penguin Random House LLC. OLIVER BAEZ BENDORF: "Rainwater from Certain Enchanted Springs" from *Advantages of Being Evergreen.* Copyright © 2019 by Oliver Baez Bendorf. Reprinted with the permission of The Permissions Company, LLC on behalf of the Cleveland State University Poetry Center, csupoetrycenter.com JAMES BROUGHTON: "only when i". In *Faeries: Visions, Voices & Pretty Dresses.* New York: Aperture,